I0077955

"*WHATEVER, GOD*"

SAINT SHENOUDA PRESS

ABOUT THE AUTHOR

Fr. Anthony Messeh is a priest in the Coptic Orthodox church, serving at the church of St. Timothy & St. Athanasius (STSA) in Arlington, Virginia. Through his blog (www.FrAnthony.com), his weekly sermons, and now through this book, Fr. Anthony brings an ancient faith to the modern world through his unique ability to communicate life-changing truths in simple and understandable ways.

"WHATEVER, GOD"

Rediscovering the One I Thought I Knew

Fr Anthony Messeh

ST SHENOUDA PRESS
SYDNEY, AUSTRALIA
2020

"*WHATEVER, GOD*"

Rediscovering the One I Thought I Knew

Fr Anthony Messeh
COPYRIGHT © 2020

St. Shenouda Press
Second Edition

All rights reserved. Except for brief quotations in critical publications or reviews, no part of this book may be reproduced in any manner without prior written permission from the publisher.

ST SHENOUDA PRESS
8419 Putty Rd
Putty, NSW, 2330
Australia

www.stshenoudapress.com
ISBN 13: 978-0-6485754-9-8

All scripture quotations, unless otherwise indicated, are taken from
the New King James Version®. Copyright © 1982 by Thomas Nelson, Inc. Used by permission. All rights reserved.

Cover Design:
Mariana Hanna
In and Out Creation Pty Ltd
inandoutcreations.com.au

CONTENTS

PART FOUR: GOD IS REWARDING 153

PART FIVE: NOW IT'S YOUR TURN 199

INTRODUCTION

THE POWER OF "WHATEVER"

"*Whatever?*"

"*Yes, Marianne, whatever,*" I said to my lovely bride-to-be. "*That's how we're going to live our lives. WHATEVER. Whatever God wants—we won't say no. No matter what He asks of us, we will do it. No matter where He takes us or what He asks of us, we'll do WHATEVER. Deal?*"

"*Deal!*" she said as we both realized the magnitude of what had just happened.

Those weren't empty words we were saying. Neither of us took that word, "*whatever,*" lightly. We both knew that we had done something big ... something hard ... something that wouldn't always make sense, but we trusted would always be best. We had just consecrated the rest of our lives to God—to go wherever, whenever, and serve however God wants. All that contained in that one little word, "*whatever.*"

That conversation, which took place 17 years ago in the sitting area of a Borders bookstore *(remember those?)*, ended up being the most important conversation of my life. How could a conversation between two young 24-year-olds, sitting in a bookstore because they were too cheap to go out to a restaurant, end up being so meaningful and life-changing?

That's what happens when you say *"whatever"* to God.

A DISCLAIMER

Please don't get the wrong impression about me from that first story. If you're thinking to yourself, *"Here comes another Christian book written by some preacher who's going to throw a whole bunch of 'Christianese' at me, and tell me to just 'surrender my life,' or 'put my trust in Jesus,' or that I need to just 'crucify my flesh' so that I can 'die to the self,' and be 'led by the Spirit,' and 'just kiss dating goodbye.'"*

If that's what you think this is going to be . . . YOU ARE WRONG! You can kiss those crazy ideas goodbye!

I'm not that guy. I've never been that guy. In fact, I don't even think I like that guy. It's just not me. I'm not the *"in your face Christian guy,"* or the *"think everyone should live in a Christian bubble"* guy, or the *"act like you got it all together and make everyone feel guilty about their messed-up lives"* kind of a guy.

That just isn't me.

I pride myself on being nothing more than an ordinary guy— an ordinary guy who lived a mostly ordinary life, but then one day I said, *"Whatever,"* and gave control of that ordinary life to an extraordinary God. I discovered firsthand the fulfillment that the word *"whatever"* can bring into your life. And my goal in writing this book is to show you what that looks like—to show you that nothing is more satisfying and more fulfilling than saying *"whatever"* to God.

That's my goal. I hope you'll give me a chance to tell my story.

PART ONE

MY STORY

CHAPTER 1

STAINED GLASS WINDOWS ON
AN EMPTY HOUSE

I wasn't always like this. I didn't used to care too much about
God. Yeah, I went to church every week *(this wasn't really
an option in my family),* and I went to Catholic school from kin-
dergarten all the way through high school. But that was about
it. That was the extent of my spiritual life—attending certain
events or classes or services, and pretty much nothing else.

I didn't have any kind of personal relationship with God. I
didn't even know what that meant *(and to be honest, I'm still
not sure I fully understand it).* I mean, I believed in God. I
thought He was a great guy and figured I should try to avoid
upsetting Him as much as I could. But that was it. It never got
any deeper than that. God wasn't really an important or active
part of my life.

To me, God wasn't really a person. *(Don't worry, you're
allowed to admit that. I just did and no lightning bolts so far.)*
God wasn't real to me. He was sort of a mix between a life
insurance policy and a good luck charm. I figured that if I just
went to church on Sunday, then when I died and was standing

3

in line to get to heaven, maybe someone up there would say, *"Yeah, I've seen him before. He looks familiar. Go ahead and let him in."*

All I wanted from God was for Him to let me into heaven when I die—and if He could somehow find a way to help me on my chemistry test, that wouldn't have hurt either. And while He was at it, if He could have somehow convinced Jessica Morgan—the most beautiful girl in high school—that I was much more fun to be with than all those boring jocks on the football team, that would have been the icing on the cake. *("Jessica Morgan" is not the girl's real name, so don't waste your time trying to find her on Facebook; my wife would KILL ME if I mentioned her real name.)*

I never really *EXPECTED* too much from God, and I guess that's why I never really *INVESTED* too much into Him either.

Well, whatever pathetic *"relationship"* I had with God when I was in high school became even more pathetic when I went away to college. I was now living on my own, away from my parents. I no longer attended a school that required me to pray in the mornings or take a class on the Bible. I didn't have to wake up early on Sunday mornings anymore to go to church. THANK GOD!

I wasn't sure if I was allowed to thank God for not having to go to church anymore, but I did it anyway—still no lightning bolts.

But not going to church started to cause a problem for me. It made me think of myself in a different way.

Everyone wants to believe that they're a good person, but I was taught that I had to go to church to be a good person. *(Catholic school education paying off here.)* So now I had a problem. I had two choices: Convince myself that I wasn't a good person? Or go to church?

I've met many people in my life, people of different backgrounds, cultures, and experiences. I've met people who've committed just about every sin there is: from adultery to drug trafficking—even murder. I know people who have done it all.

But I've never met a person who wants to think of himself as a bad person. The human psyche can't take that. We'll do whatever we can to convince ourselves that we're good—even if it means going to church!

So, I decided to go.

I found a church that had services on Saturday evenings from 5:15 to 6:00 p.m. 45 minutes? Are you kidding me? That's it?

Back home, church services were an all-day event! The service was two to three hours long, and then there was another hour for Sunday school, and then another hour trying to find my mom, and telling her to stop talking and *"LET'S GO HOME!"* But the church service I discovered at school was only 45 minutes long—38 minutes when you factored in that I was the last one to arrive and the first one to leave. Even I could do that. And the services weren't in the morning! They were conveniently scheduled on Saturdays after football games and before the night life began. Now that's how you attract college students! It was perfect—at least for me.

But looking back, it was quite possibly the worst thing for me. I would've been better off not going to any church and accepting the truth THAT I HAD ZERO CONNECTION TO GOD.

I was living away from God; I was doing my own thing. I was just decorating the outside of my life with some spiritual practices, but the truth is the inside was hollow, like stained glass windows on an empty house. Instead of seeing the truth, I did what we all do: I deceived myself.

5

I convinced myself that I was good because I went to a church service once a week for 38 minutes. That's it.

But the truth is I wasn't fine; I wasn't good—not even close. I was in the worst possible place—a place of SELF DECEPTION. But God has a way of making you realize the truth, doesn't He? It's called "life," and it was coming for me.

THE HOUSE COMES CRASHING DOWN

Life happened during my third year of college. My family went through some personal struggles and it really hit us/me hard. It wasn't anything between my parents or anything like that; thankfully, they've been happily married for close to 50 years now. It was a situation that thrust itself upon my family, and we had to face it together.

Actually, they had to face it together without me. I was still away at college and that shielded me from a lot of the physical pain they endured. But that only made the emotional pain worse because I felt like I couldn't do anything to help.

Now realize that I'm about as unemotional a guy as there is on the planet. If you don't believe me, ask my wife—or try watching a romantic comedy movie with me. According to my wife, it's about as unenjoyable an experience as you can imagine. I'm just not that emotional. I don't cry. I don't get shaken. That stuff doesn't happen to me.

But this situation shook me. It shook me hard. It even made me cry . . . a lot!

Looking back, the reason it hit me so hard was because I had nothing to fall back on. I had no support network. I had nothing solid on which to stand.

My friends weren't going to help me get through it. Yeah, we were friends, and I loved hanging out with them, but that's about it. We were guys. We didn't talk about stuff—especially serious stuff or personal stuff. Those two forms of stuff were off limits. We just hung out and played basketball and watched *The Simpsons*. That's it.

My parents were always there for me, but they were in the middle of the fire. I was the one on the outside, and I felt it was my responsibility to be strong for them.

So where could I turn? I wanted to turn to God, but I didn't even know what that meant. I didn't have a real relationship with Him. All I knew how to do was go to church and not do bad stuff. But I was struggling and I needed help. Where could I find it?

I then did the only thing I could think of doing: I started praying. Sincere praying. Not just saying words, but really praying from my heart—sometimes with tears too. I didn't know what I was supposed to say, but I just said whatever I felt. I wasn't praying because I had to or because I was sup-posed to . . . I was praying because I needed God—I really, really needed God.

Those prayers were special; I still remember some of them. It's those *"broken heart"* prayers that are the most powerful. I've heard it said that *"the heart that's soaked with tears is the most fertile place for prayers to grow."* That was my experi-ence during that time.

That time wasn't easy. It was one of the toughest times of my life—a time so tough that I remember on more than one occasion crying in the car while driving back to school after a weekend at home. But it was that tough time that led to those prayers.

And it was those prayers that led to a miracle . . .

CHAPTER 2

MONEY AND GIRLS: MY SPIRITUAL LIFE BEGINS

*I*t was the summer of 1997—the summer before my final year of college. I was riding high because I was able to land a real job that summer, working as an intern with a big telecommunications company. It was the first non-hourly job of my life, and I was excited!

Ironically, I was hired by someone I knew from church—the church that I went to back home. The guy who hired me was quite involved there, he knew my parents well, and I think he only agreed to hire me because I was their son. But I didn't really care; I just wanted the money and the experience.

Getting that job pushed me to be more active at church. The guy thought he was hiring a good church boy, so the least I could do was put him at ease about that. And that was the first thing God did to draw me closer to Him that summer.

The second thing God did is something that I can't believe I'm about to write. You can't see me, but trust me, I am cringing right now because I know what you're about to read.

I'm a priest. An ordained clergyman. A man of the cloth. A man of God. So logically, what would be one of the main factors that drew me closer to God and closer to church when I was just a young lad in college?

Yep . . . you guessed it . . . A GIRL!

Not just a girl, though. I'd be lying if I just said I met a girl and that was it. The truth is I didn't just meet a girl— *(this is so embarrassing and sounds so bad)*—I met a girl on Good Friday . . . in the parking lot . . . after I skipped the entire service.

Now I'm really starting to worry about those lightning bolts.

I know, I know, I know. It sounds so awful, and looks even more awful in writing. I told you, I was very shallow at the time, and my relationship with God was superficial. I came to church on Good Friday *(ironically, the first Good Friday I can even remember),* went in and out of the service a few times, and then as I was leaving, I spotted the kind of girl that I didn't know existed at my church . . . A BEAUTIFUL ONE!

So now—between the job and the girl—I had plenty of reasons to be at church a lot that summer. And I was. Friday nights, Saturday nights, day trips, playing basketball, watching movies, hanging out in the parking lot—even when the girl wasn't around.

And just for the record, while it was that girl who initially caught my eye and *drew* me to church, that was only at the start. I never had more than a one-minute conversation with her, and to this day the only one who knows her identity is my wife. *(So yeah, in case you were wondering if the mystery girl turns out to be my wife, the answer is no. But that sure would make this story easier to tell if it was!)*

9

Slowly but surely God did a miracle. He drew me closer to Him. And He did so in a very *creative* way. *(Money and girls— isn't that how all priests get their start?)*

God had watched me live my whole life without Him. But now that the going had gotten tough, He knew I needed Him. He couldn't just leave me out there alone. He needed to step in.

Just as a father respects his son who says, *"Leave me alone, Dad—I want to try to ride this bike by myself,"* God respected my wishes and let me try to do it on my own. But what would the father do if he saw his boy in trouble? Would he stand there and watch him fall? No! No dad would do that. No dad would leave his son to seriously injure himself when it was in his power to save him.

That's how God dealt with me. He respected my wish to try to do it on my own; He let me do it that way for the first 20 years of my life. He knew that I couldn't do it for very long, but He never forced Himself upon me; He respected my wishes.

But that was before. Now things had become serious. Now I was in trouble. As I mentioned in the last chapter, I really, really needed God. I needed help. I had nowhere to turn. And God saw that, and He did what He always does: He found a way. He found a way to draw me closer to Him.

They say that sometimes God needs to knock you flat on your back to get you to look up. That's what happened to me. And yes, the main characters in the story might have appeared to be a girl and a job, but the Author and Director of the story was none other than God Himself.

FALLING IN LOVE WITH GOD

The summer of 1997 passed, and it was a pivotal one. That summer set me on a new course of life—one where God was no longer a stranger, but someone that I started to understand a little more. I still didn't fully get it, but I knew that when I was close to God, I felt better. Life seemed better. I liked where this was going.

The situation with my family wasn't resolved *(it was actually only getting started)*, but somehow the more time we spent at church, and in church services, and with church people *(not the girl)*, the better we felt. God didn't solve our problem, but He did comfort us and strengthen us during the ordeal in an undeniable way.

I didn't know much, but I knew that I wanted more of God in my life.

So, I did something crazy—something that to this day I can't comprehend why I did it, or what pushed me to make such a decision. I booked a ticket to spend five weeks in Africa the following summer on a mission trip to Kenya, Tanzania, and Uganda.

The reason I say this was so crazy is because, to this day, I have no idea why I went on this trip. I had never been to Africa before. I didn't know anyone who was going on the trip. There was a group of 12 to 15 young people from other churches going, but I didn't know any of them. They were coming from Los Angeles and New York and Houston and Montreal. I had never met any of them. I didn't know where I was going, or what I'd be doing when I got there, or whom I'd be doing it with.

But for some reason, I did it. I booked the ticket and went. And . . .

. . . those five weeks changed my life forever.

This book is too short for me to write about all that happened or all I witnessed during that trip to Africa. But I will say this: *I fell in love with God there*.

It was during those five weeks that God became real to me. He was no longer a "thing" or an "it." Starting in Africa, God became a real person. He was my Father. He was someone who cared about me deeply, and someone who wanted to be intimately involved in my life.

I never knew that before. I never knew that God wanted more than a weekly status report of my life. He didn't want me to just check in once a week; He wanted more. He wanted a relationship—a real one . . . a living one . . . one that goes two ways, not just one.

And the best thing I realized was that this relationship wasn't something that God wanted *FROM me,* but rather something He wanted *FOR me*. There's a big difference.

I was the one who would be the primary beneficiary, not Him. He didn't need me; I needed Him. All these years I had thought I was doing God a favor by going to church . . . by praying before I went to bed . . . by avoiding those pesky four-letter words. I thought I was doing it for Him. But man, was I wrong! God doesn't want those things for His sake; He wants them for my sake! He's not the beneficiary—I am!

When God becomes a part of your life, everything looks different. Everything tastes different. Everything has new meaning and is fresh. That's what I experienced in Africa, and from then on, life was never the same. I fell in love with God, and I was ready and willing to do whatever God wanted me to do.

When I came home from that trip, the same spirit continued. I became very involved at church—not just attending church, but volunteering and serving in any way I could. I led Bible studies. I started a sandwich run for the homeless in DC. I taught Sunday school. I drove the church van. I even cleaned the church trash cans! You name it, I did it. I never said no to anything.

I wanted to do anything and everything I could to get closer to God. I was all in, fully committed, sold-out, on fire for God, and I was going to stay this way forever!

Or so I thought . . .

CHAPTER 3

THERE'S A HOLE IN THE BOAT

"Let him who thinks he stands take heed lest he fall."
(1 Corinthians 10:12)

*T*here's a lot of wisdom in those 11 words, as I soon found out.

After my *"falling in love"* summer of 1998, I thought I was on top of the world. Yeah, I still had my shortcomings and flaws, but for the most part, I was living the kind of life that I thought would make God proud. I wasn't just active in church, but I was sincere in my personal devotion as well.

I prayed as often as I could—going so far as even to sneak away from my desk at work and stand at the bottom of a stairwell to get a few minutes of private prayer in during the workday. I carried my Bible with me everywhere I went and was always looking for a few moments to read the next chapter. I got very involved in the ministry at my church and began serving with the utmost dedication and commitment.

I was living the kind of life that you'd expect from someone who would end up becoming a priest. But there was a problem . . . I had a hole in the boat.

A hole in the boat? You've heard the saying *"It only takes a spark to get a fire going,"* right? Well, how about this one: *"It only takes a small leak to sink a mighty ship."*

In other words, no matter how *"good"* you may think you are, or how devoted to God your life might seem to be, it doesn't take much to trip you up and knock you flat on your face—especially if you don't see it coming!

That's what happened to me. Without going into too much detail, I'll say this: The devil *(the enemy of God and of all God's children)* was watching me grow, and watching me pray, and watching me get closer to God. He was watching and waiting— waiting for just the right time to stick his leg out and trip me up and make me come crashing down.

And that's exactly what he did.

The details aren't important—all that's important is that the devil got me, and he got me good. He got me to fall into a sin, which I never saw coming. And when it hit me, it hit me hard. It made me question everything about myself and my relationship with God.

Did I really have a relationship with God or was this all just a show? Was any of this real? Were my prayers real? Did I ever really connect with God or was this all just my imagination? Am I really a better person than I was before I started all this? If I am, how could I have fallen so badly? Could God still make something good out of my life after I did this?

Needless to say, I was confused. I was struggling with doubt. My relationship with God had grown, but I was still pretty new to this whole thing and this was the first major storm I experienced in my walk with God.

I didn't know what to do. I needed help. I wanted to turn to God, but I didn't know if I could anymore. I lost that right when I disobeyed Him, didn't I? Even if I did go to God, how would I be able to decipher His voice? My head was so filled with confusion that I couldn't think clearly.

I needed help, and I could think of only one place to find it: Father Bishoy.

Father Bishoy was the priest at my church. I had only known him for a couple of years at the time since he had only been at our church since the spring of 1997—just before I started making my comeback to church. Truth be told, he was instrumental in my return to God because he took me under his wing. He guided me and taught me the ins and outs of the spiritual life, and without his guidance, I don't know where I'd be today.

So, I went to him. I told him everything. I cried. I don't think he cried, but he looked like he was close *(or at least that's how I interpreted it)*. He looked disappointed; I felt like I had let him down. I was supposed to be a leader in the church and in the ministry; he had trusted me to do a lot. But how could I continue in that position after what I had done? I couldn't . . . could I?

Deep in my heart, I felt something telling me that I just needed to get away. I needed to start over. I needed to go to a new place where I could start fresh and build my spiritual life the right way—one step at a time. I felt I needed to move to a new city, and even a new state.

So I said it. I told Father Bishoy that I think I should leave Virginia and move elsewhere.

And to my surprise, he agreed. I didn't think he'd agree in a million years. I thought he was going to say, *"No, you're overreacting, don't worry, just relax and everything will be fine."*

But he didn't. He agreed. He said I should move away.

Now, let me just pause the story for a moment here and explain that I had no idea what I was saying when I suggested that I move away. With the exception of the first 18 months of my life, I had lived in Virginia my entire life. I was born in New Jersey, but we moved to Virginia when I was less than two years old, and I had been there ever since. Even when I went away to college, I didn't go far. I went to the University of Virginia, just two hours south of my home in Northern Virginia.

Virginia was all I knew. I didn't know how to live anywhere else, and I'd never had a reason to even consider it. All I had was this gut feeling that God wanted me to move away.

But now—after that conversation with Father Bishoy—I had more than that. I had confirmation from my spiritual father. I had to go.

I walked out of that meeting and thought to myself, *"I don't know how or why or where, but God, if you want me to go, I will go."*

And that night, I started developing my escape plan.

MY ABRAHAM MOMENT

I'm not an impulsive person by any means. I am more Type A than my story suggests. I know I've had a lot of impulsive-looking episodes in my story thus far, but trust me, that's not who I am.

I'm a planner. I like lists . . . lists with bullet points . . . lists with bullet points that I can check off as I get them done. Nothing's better than checking stuff off a list!

I don't like winging it. I don't like "flying by the seat of my pants" or figuring it out along the way, *(or if you're spiritual, you call it "being led by the Spirit")*.

That's just not me.

So how does someone who likes to plan and be well-prepared end up deciding to move to another state in just one night?

That's God!

I can't explain it, but I'm telling you, I was 100% certain that God wanted me to move. I had the strongest feeling in my gut saying, *"You need to leave. If you love Me, you need to get out of here and move away."* And I even felt like I knew where God wanted me to go . . . North Carolina.

Why North Carolina? No good reason, *(but then again, I didn't really have a good reason why I was leaving in the first place, so why would I need a good reason to decide where I was going?).*

I'd never been to North Carolina, nor did I know anyone who lived there. That was a plus for me. I wanted a fresh start. I wanted to be alone. I wanted to go to a place where no one knew me. So North Carolina made sense in that regard. It would have been nice if I'd had a job lined up there, but I didn't really care about that at the time.

Why? Because again, this wasn't a decision I was making, but rather a command I was obeying. I wasn't going to North Carolina because it made sense, I was going because God told me to go. And I decided that I was going to obey God, no matter how crazy it sounded. And the craziness was just beginning.

The first thing I did was go to my boss. I needed to tell him that I was leaving. At the time, I was working for a small IT consulting firm, and I'd been there for about two years.

I didn't know what I was going to say. I assumed he was going to ask me why I was resigning, and I didn't really have a reason—at least not one that he'd understand. What could I say? *"I'm quitting to move to North Carolina, even though I don't have a job or a house or even a single friend in the entire state"?* Not exactly the best way to leave the door open for a rehire in case I ever came back. He was going to think I was nuts!

But again, I didn't care. This wasn't about making a career move; this was about doing what God told me to do.

So I did it. I told him I was leaving. As expected he asked, *"Why?"* I told him I was moving for personal reasons. *(Once you say personal reasons, everyone leaves you alone.)* But when I told him I was going to North Carolina, he asked me, *"Where in North Carolina?"*

Now I really felt like an idiot because I honestly had no idea. I had heard of a few cities in North Carolina, but I didn't really have any idea where I'd be going. The one city I knew was Chapel Hill *(home of the University of North Carolina)*. The only reason I knew it was because I was a huge Michael Jordan fan and that's where he played college basketball.

So I said, *"Uh . . . hmmm . . . well, I'm not really sure exactly where quite yet, but most likely it'll be somewhere in the Chapel Hill area."*

I thought that sounded pretty good. Either way, I didn't really care what he thought about me. I was quitting anyway, so what did it matter . . . or so I thought.

What he said next shocked me.

"Chapel Hill, huh? That's actually not too far from our Raleigh office. Would you be interested in seeing if we could work out a transfer to get you into that office?"

I was planning to move down there with no job, and finding something when I got there. *(The job market was much different back in 2000 than it is today.)* But unbeknownst to me, my small IT consulting firm was in the process of being bought out by a large IT consulting company, and that large company needed consultants to work out of the Raleigh office.

I thought, *"Are you kidding me?"* I felt God saying, *"You're doing the right thing; keep going."*

And so I did.

The next thing I needed to do was tell my parents. As expected, they were very confused by my announcement. To their credit, even though I know it hurt them, they never tried to stand in my way. They were always 100% supportive, even though they didn't understand or agree with my reasoning for leaving. They stood by me and supported me the whole way.

Now all I needed was a place to stay. I made plans to drive down to Raleigh one weekend to go apartment shopping. I had money saved up. I knew where the company office was located. I'd done my research and I knew the exact area where I wanted to live. It should have been simple.

I arrived in Raleigh and wasted no time. I looked at two or three different apartments and was ready to make my decision. I negotiated a good deal and told the lady that I was ready to sign a one-year lease and move in the next month.

Now at that time, the situation with my job wasn't fully settled yet. We were still working out the details, and the week before my trip to Raleigh, things were looking like they might NOT go as smoothly as we had originally thought. But to be honest, that didn't deter me. I kept reminding myself, *"I'm not going for the job; I'm going for God. Period."*

So, I asked for the paperwork for the lease. I filled it out and wrote a check for the deposit. I was 100% in, and I was doing what God had told me to do . . .

. . . Not quite. The lady at the leasing office told me that she needed some more paperwork from me. I don't recall now what was missing, but apparently it was something important, because she wouldn't let me sign the lease without it. She said, *"I'm sorry, sir, but we can't make it official until we get that paperwork."*

Not a big deal. I told her I would mail it on Monday when I got back home. She told me to keep my deposit check and mail it in with the paperwork.

All righty! No big deal. Just a minor delay, but nothing had really changed, right?

That's what I thought, but I soon discovered that actually *EVERYTHING had changed.*

I got back to work on Monday, and my boss called me into his office. The job transfer wasn't going to work out after all; it had fallen through. If I wanted to leave Virginia, I would have to resign.

What's going on here, God? Why aren't You helping me? I am doing this for You, not me. What happened, God?

I was confused. I still felt like I was supposed to go to North Carolina, but all of a sudden, I wasn't so sure. That job thing made me question everything. I was still fully determined to obey God, but now I wasn't sure that leaving was still what God wanted.

How could I be sure? Back to Father Bishoy.

I told him the whole story, and he confirmed what I was once again feeling in my gut: God didn't really want me to leave. He was just testing me. He wanted to see if I would obey Him or not. He wanted to know what was really in my heart.

There's a famous story in the Bible about a guy named Abraham. It's one of my absolute favorite stories. In it, God challenges Abraham to do something crazy, something so crazy that no one in his right mind could have justified it. He asked Abraham to sacrifice his own son.

"Take now your son, your only son Isaac, whom you love, and go to the land of Moriah, and offer him there as a burnt offering on one of the mountains of which I shall tell you." (Genesis 22:2)

Now that's crazy! Why would God do that? Why would God ask Abraham to do something so hard?

Abraham didn't know the answer. God didn't tell him WHY; He only told him WHAT.

And Abraham obeyed.

Then they came to the place of which God had told him. And Abraham built an altar there and placed the wood in order; and he bound Isaac his son and laid him on the altar, upon the wood. And Abraham stretched out his hand and took the knife to slay his son. (Genesis 22:9-10)

Can you picture it? Can you see Abraham at the top of the mountain, with his son Isaac tied to an altar of wood? When I picture it, I see Isaac with his eyes closed, and he's bracing himself for the unthinkable. His father Abraham, who loves him so dearly, has a knife in his hand, and he's raising that knife towards the sky. He's getting ready to plunge it into his son's body. Picture the scene and imagine the agony in Abraham's heart.

Just then—right when Abraham is about to thrust the knife and take his son's life—God intervenes.

> But the Angel of the Lord called to him from heaven
> and said, "Abraham, Abraham!" So he said, "Here I
> am." And He said, "Do not lay your hand on the lad,
> or do anything to him; for now I know that you fear
> God, since you have not withheld your son, your
> only son, from Me." (Genesis 22:11-12)

God stopped Abraham at the last possible second. Abraham didn't realize it at the time, but God never really wanted him to kill his son; God just wanted to test his heart. He wanted to see what Abraham was really made of. Would Abraham withhold his son from God? Or would he be willing to let go of Isaac if God asked him to?

Once God saw what was in Abraham's heart, God made a special promise to him, a promise that is unlike any promise He's ever made to anyone else.

> "By Myself I have sworn," says the Lord, "because
> you have done this thing, and have not withheld your
> son, your only son—blessing I will bless you, and
> multiplying I will multiply your descendants as the
> stars of the heaven and as the sand which is on the
> seashore; and your descendants shall possess the
> gate of their enemies. In your seed all the nations of
> the earth shall be blessed, because you have obeyed
> My voice." (Genesis 22:16-18)

This was my "Abraham moment"—not that what I did was anywhere near what he did. But this was my test. This was where God challenged me to do something crazy, something that made no sense and would cause me and my loved ones a lot of pain. He knew this would be hard, but He asked me to do it anyway.

23

And He did that not to hurt me, but rather to test me—to see what was in my heart.

Abraham was tested. I was tested. Abraham was ready to sacrifice everything. I was ready to sacrifice everything. Abraham was blessed immensely. Would I be blessed as well?

The answer was coming . . . on November 2, 2000.

CHAPTER 4

HERE COMES THE BLESSING

*N*ovember 2, 2000: a day that will go down in the history books. That day is up there with 1) the day I got married, 2) the day my children were born, and 3) the day the New England Patriots lost Super Bowl XLII to the New York Giants. *(I'm not really a Giants fan, but man, I hated those Patriots back in 2007; they beat my beloved Washington Redskins 52-7 in the regular season, and that is what happens when you run up the score on God's favorite team!)*

Back to November 2. That was the day that I found myself sitting in a Fuddruckers restaurant with my future wife, Marianne. That night was so special, and to me, it was the beginning of the greatest blessing in my life.

Marianne and I had known each other our whole lives. Our parents were friends since forever. Our dads actually went to college together back in Egypt; they both immigrated to the United States around the same time. My family came to New Jersey *(where I was born in late August 1976)* and Marianne's family went to California *(where she was born just 13 days later)*.

We both ended up in Virginia, though, and our lives were connected ever since. We went to the same elementary school — where apparently I was her first crush in fifth grade. *(This shows that she was clearly a smart girl, full of wisdom from even a young age.)* We both attended Catholic high schools in the same area, and then both ended up at the University of Virginia for our college years.

So we knew a lot about each other. But you know what was interesting about our relationship? WE WERE NEVER FRIENDS. We knew each other at an acquaintance level, and she was a friend of the family, but our relationship was never anything beyond that.

But that all changed on November 2, 2000. By then, I was in a whole new place. I felt like I needed a companion in life — someone who shared the same passion and love for God that I did. I needed someone who would help me live a life that is pleasing to God, someone who would understand that God comes first in our lives, and where He leads, we will follow. I needed a partner . . . a teammate.

And when I thought about it that way, it was a no-brainer. Marianne was the one. She was the one who could help me get to where God wanted me to be. She was the most godly and God-fearing girl I knew. SHE WAS THE ONE!

Now I just needed to convince her of that.

Like I said, we had known each other our whole lives, but we weren't really friends. In fact, when we were kids and her family would come to our house, my brothers and I made sure that she and her sister felt as uncomfortable as possible.

Why? Because they were girls! Why would we want to play with girls? We didn't have girl toys and we didn't do girl stuff. We did boy stuff — like watching wrestling, or playing with our action figures *(not dolls, action figures!)*, or competing in video games as if our lives depended on it. That's what boys did.

But now things had changed. I wanted to ask her out, but I worried that it would be really awkward because even though we'd known each other for so long, we'd barely spoken to each other. This definitely was going to be weird, but sometimes you gotta roll the dice.

So, I asked her out. I emailed her and told her I was going to be in her area that night, and I wanted to see if she wanted to grab dinner at Fuddruckers. She said yes.

I approached the night the way I approach just about everything in life: like a mission. I was a solider and I had a job to do. My plan was to meet Marianne, tell her I wanted to start dating, eat a fish burger, and then go home. 1-2-3. Very straightforward. That was my plan. *(I told you I was Type A.)*

And the night started according to my plan. We arrived at the restaurant, we made small talk for a few minutes, and then we ordered. Once the food came, we said a short prayer over the food. And then I went for the kill.

"Marianne, you're probably wondering why I invited you out to dinner. Well, I have really been feeling that now is the time for me to start thinking seriously about marriage. I want to start moving in that direction, and after praying about it, I feel like God is pushing me to pursue a relationship with you—not just for casual dating, but to see if this could lead to marriage. That is why I invited you here. I wanted to see if you're interested. What do you think?"

You may think I'm joking, but that's the honest to goodness truth. That's what I said. And I said it the moment we finished praying. No intro. No easing into it. No beating around the bush. Straightforward. Direct. And about as unromantic as you can get!

Now it was time for Marianne to respond. Before I tell you how she did respond, let me give you a chance to guess. Did she say:

a) *"Ha! Yeah right! We ain't in fifth grade no more, Jack! I knew you were going to ask me out, and I just brought you here to humiliate you for all those years of making me watch you and your brothers play with your stupid wrestling dolls while my sister and I sat there bored to death! And yes, they're dolls! Not action figures!!!"*

b) *"Yes, that seems like a well-thought-out and reasonable idea. I commend you on the brevity and succinctness with which you presented your proposition. I agree."*

c) *"WOO-HOO!!!!!!!! My dream come true! I've been waiting for this day since fifth grade. In my book, it's always been Tom Cruise, then Kevin Costner, then you!"*

The truth is she didn't respond in any of those ways (although C was probably the closest, I'd say). What she did instead was something completely different.

She started talking . . .

. . . and talking . . .

. . . and talking . . .

Once she started talking, I started eating. She kept talking; I kept eating. I don't remember everything she said, but I do remember finishing my sandwich, and then my fries, and then interrupting her to see if she was going to eat her pickle.

And during this whole time, she was still talking! What was she saying? A LOT!

She said how she really felt God had prepared her for this, and then went on to explain why. She said that there were other guys who had recently expressed an interest in her, but she never felt at peace about any of them, and she didn't know why. She said how she felt very overwhelmed by God's goodness and love for her.

My response? *(I promise you I'm not lying here.)* "That's really great, Marianne. So is that a YES or a NO?"

I can't tell you how often Marianne and I look back on this moment and laugh our heads off. She pours out her heart and tells me her life story; I devour my burger and fries, and then ask, *"Are you saying yes or no?"* HYSTERICAL!

Well, after she got past the fact that I wasn't joking, and that I really had no clue if she was saying yes or no, she spelled it out to me in plain language. She said YES! We both agreed that we were interested in pursuing this relationship to see if it was from God or not. We agreed that we would seek God's guidance and obey His will—even if that meant going against our own wills. In other words, we'd grow together as long as we both felt that God wanted that. But we'd always be prepared that God could ask us to end it at any moment, and if that was the case, we wouldn't say no.

This relationship was not about us, it was about God. It wasn't me telling Him, *"I want to marry this girl."* I really felt it was Him saying, *"I want you to marry this girl."* And there's a big difference between the two.

We started dating, and God's Hand was evident in our relationship from the start. We both felt very good about what was happening, but we still stayed committed to praying, *"God, we*

29

love each other and we want to be together. But if you want us to break up for any reason, we won't say no. We don't want that, and that would break our hearts, but we'll never say no to You. Just speak to us loud and clear, Lord, and we will obey."

Remember, I'd already had my Abraham moment, so I knew how this worked. God can't bless what you don't surrender to Him; the only way to get God's blessing is to put it in His Hands.

So surrendering is what we did. And blessing is what He GAVE!

Our first date was in November 2000; our wedding was in May 2001. Six months. That's all it took for us to realize that God was in this relationship and that He had a plan for us—a special plan that was much bigger than either one of us.

> "For I know the plans I have for you," declares the LORD, "plans to prosper you and not to harm you, plans to give you hope and a future." (Jeremiah 29:11)

God's plan was moving forward. We were both on cloud nine. We could feel His blessing in a very real and tangible way. And it was the greatest feeling ever.

There was just one thing left to do before sealing the deal . . . one conversation we still needed to have.

CHAPTER 5

THE CONVERSATION THAT DEFINED MY LIFE

*F*ast forward to March 2001. We're now two months out from the wedding, and we're sitting in a Borders bookstore where we went regularly for our dates. Why pay money for dinner when all I was really interested in was the company? *(FYI, guys, that line works only once or twice, so use sparingly.)* We were sitting, enjoying our complimentary cups of water, and then Marianne asked, *"Are you going to become a priest after we get married?"*

She asked this question because that's what people were saying. There was no plan for me to become a priest — no discussion about the topic. But I guess people just like to make predictions. *(This isn't just my church, is it?)*

Now, to fully appreciate this story, you need to see the full context.

I didn't fit the prototype of a typical priest. I had only been actively involved in church for about three to four years now, and during that time, I had never seen anyone make the transformation from ordinary person to priest. I thought that priests just kind of "came out of the box" that way. I pictured them as quiet, little kids with black robes and beards, sitting inside during recess so they could read their Bibles and not defile themselves with the regular kids who played football and basketball and other sports. And in that picture, I definitely fit more with the normal kids outside vs. the *"priest"* kids inside.

I thought priesthood wasn't for people like me. I'd serve God somehow and someway, but not as a priest.

But that's why my next statement was so important.

"Marianne, you want to know what I think about priesthood? If I wanted to be a priest with all my heart, I wouldn't take one step towards it. And if I didn't want to be a priest with all my heart, I wouldn't take one step away from it. WHATEVER GOD SAYS, I WILL DO."

That was the defining moment of my life, that conversation. We laid it all out on the line together and agreed that whatever God wanted, we would do. We wouldn't say no. We'd never say no. If He wants priesthood, we won't say no.

If He wants us to go to Africa and serve as missionaries *(which at the time is where both of us thought God was leading us)*, we won't say no.

If He wants us to work making minimum wage, we won't say no.

And, worst-case scenario, if God wants us to continue working as IT consultants *(that's what she also was doing at the time)*, we won't say no. We might not like it, and we might pray with all our hearts that He has something greater in store for us, but we won't ever say no.

No matter what God requests of us, we will say, *"Whatever."*

THE REST OF THE STORY

That conversation changed my life. After that, everything was easy. The hard part was the decision, but once that was made, everything else flowed from there.

Eventually we got married, and it was the greatest and most glorious wedding I'd ever been too. In addition to all the planned speeches at the reception, we had two *"impromptu"* speeches (sermons) given by the two clergy in attendance: Father Bishoy and Bishop Paul, the missionary bishop who dedicated his life to serving God in Africa, and who helped me fall in love with God during my time there in 1998.

They each spoke about the blessing of God that comes to those who wait for Him and obey His commands. We knew these messages were not only from them, but rather from God, and we received them as such.

Later that same year, Father Bishoy told me that he wanted me to become a priest and serve alongside him at the church I had grown up in. I always joke with Father Bishoy that to this day I still haven't said yes to that request. But it wasn't a request; he didn't ask me my opinion. He kind of told me, *"This is what is going to happen,"* and I didn't say anything. I didn't ask any questions. I just said okay, and that was that.

People always ask, *"How could you make such a big decision at so young an age? Was it hard?"*

My response is simple. I didn't make any decision that day. The decision was made much earlier—back in the Borders bookstore. That was when I surrendered control to God. That was the day I said, *"Whatever, God."* From then on, it may not have always been easy, but it sure was simple.

God says GO; I say YES. Never easy, but always simple.

And now I'm doing what I think is the craziest thing of all
. . . I'M WRITING A BOOK!

How crazy is that? Go tell my former high school English
teachers, and they'll laugh you out of the room.

I remember taking a writing class my first year at the
University of Virginia. The classes were small (8 to 12 people)
and I ended up with an 8 a.m. class.

Students, pay close attention here: If you're going to sign
up for an 8 a.m. class, make sure that it has more than 12
people in it. Why? Because when there are only 12 people in
the room, it becomes a lot harder to hide the fact that you are
dead asleep. TRUST ME!

Bottom line: I don't know why I'm writing a book.

Oh yes I do . . . I'm writing a book because God wants me to
write a book and I can't say no. *(That one gets me every time.)*

I could list 50 reasons why I shouldn't be writing this book:
I don't know what I'm doing . . . it's going to stink . . . I don't
have time . . . it's going to stink even more because I don't have
the time to make it not stink . . . and so on and so forth.

I wish I could say that I have great faith that this book is
going to be a best-seller, and I'm going to be a top author one
day, but truth be told, I don't. I don't have much faith in myself
or in my ability to write. But I do have faith in God and that
He called me to write this book; so therefore, its success is ultimately up to Him, not me.

My job is just to obey and share my story and the lessons
that I've learned along the way.

My goal is to show you that a life lived for God is the best
choice you can ever make. It was for me. It won't be the easiest
choice you can make, nor will it always be the most popular,
but I guarantee it will be the most rewarding.

For years I was just *"going through the motions"* — Christian in name, but not much more than that. I believed in God, but I didn't have a real relationship with Him. He wasn't a real part of my life. He was just up there somewhere, and I was down here, and that was pretty much it.

But then I tasted something different. I saw that there's so much more—so much more that God wants FOR me, not FROM me. He has a plan for my life . . . no, not a plan, but rather a DREAM! And that dream is something that is much greater than you can possibly imagine.

> Eye has not seen, nor ear heard, nor have entered into the heart of man the things which God has prepared for those who love Him. (1 Corinthians 2:9)

My goal is to show you what that life can look like, and help you take a step or two to get there. If there's one thing that I believe very passionately, it's this: GOD HAS A PLAN FOR YOUR LIFE.

He had a plan for my life, but I just couldn't see it all those years. It wasn't until I accepted His plan—even though I didn't know what it would contain at the time—that He started to reveal it to me. And I'd be lying if I said I've got it all figured out now. Not even close! God will continue to unveil more and more of His plan as long as I continue to say *"whatever"* to it.

I believe God has a unique plan for your life, too. That's why I wrote this book. My purpose isn't to teach you everything you need to know, but rather to share everything I know. My goal is to help you see where God wants you to be . . . how He wants you to live . . . and what your life should look like and could look like if you allow Him to lead it for you.

If you just say, *"Whatever."*

CHAPTER 6

THE GOD I NEVER KNEW

*T*he purpose of this book is to help you understand three important lessons that I didn't know for years.

God is REAL. God is RELEVANT. God is REWARDING.

For years, I didn't know that. I must have been absent the day they taught that in school. I didn't know that I could relate to God the same way I relate to a person . . . a friend . . . a father. I didn't know that God is real and that He desires a personal relationship with me.

I also didn't know that God is relevant. I used to think of Him as just some kind of all-powerful and almighty being who rules the universe the same way a 9-year-old rules over his ant farm, watching it when He's bored and shaking it up every now and then for fun. But nothing could be further from the truth.

God wants to be actively involved in your life. He wants to show you that He is relevant to your circumstances, no matter what they may be. If you're weak, He has strength. If you're confused, He has wisdom. If you're stressed, He has peace. If you're lost, He has the way . . . no, actually, He is the way. Whatever your circumstances, God is relevant.

And lastly, I definitely didn't know that a life with God is rewarding . . . so rewarding . . . infinitely rewarding. And that reward isn't just in heaven; it's here on earth as well. Nothing is more fulfilling than an intimate relationship with the Creator of the universe and the Lover of our souls.

In short, the purpose of this book is to show you that a life lived *WITH God* and *FOR God* is the best choice you'll ever make. It was for me. I've been on both sides. I've been through the *"don't-get-too-close-to-God-because-He-might-ruin-your-life"* phase. I lived there for years, keeping God at arm's length, and trying to keep Him from getting too close. I've also been through the *"I-can't-get-enough-of-God-in-my-life"* phase — fully devoted to God and doing everything I could to obey Him and serve His purpose.

There's no comparison. Life with God beats life without God by a landslide every time. It won't always be the easiest, but I promise you that it will be the most satisfying.

My goal in this book is to help you see what that life looks like, and what steps you can take to get there.

Growing up, I thought God was complex, far away, difficult to understand, and impossible to relate to. I pictured Him as more of a manager of the universe, instead of the Lover of mankind.

But what I've learned is that I was wrong.

God isn't far away; He is near.

God doesn't sit idle as the world turns and you live your life; He is actively involved in ways that you'll never realize.

And finally, God isn't just here to make your life miserable and give you a bunch of rules to follow; He is here to guide you to the path of joy and fulfillment—the kind that this world can never give you.

Simply put: The purpose of this book is to show you that *God is REAL, God is RELEVANT, and God is REWARDING.*

Welcome to my book.

PART TWO

GOD IS REAL

"The most telling characteristic about a man is what his view of God is. This will determine the outcome of his life more than anything else." ~Author Unknown

*T*rue story. Once upon a time, there was a young man named Andy and a young woman named Julie *(names changed to protect the innocent)*. Andy and Julie had known each other their whole lives. They grew up in the same town, went to the same school, and even attended the same church. Their families were friends, their siblings were friends, and even their friends were friends. Everyone was friends except them!

Andy didn't care much for Julie. In his mind, she was arrogant and stuck up. Yeah, she was kind of pretty, but his attraction to her appearance was outweighed by his disdain for her demeanor. Julie always seemed a bit standoffish whenever Andy was around and, understandably, that turned him off.

What made it worse for Andy was that no one else seemed to see this side of Julie. Everyone always spoke so highly of her. *"She's so sweet,"* or *"She's so friendly,"* or *"She's the best, isn't she?"* But Andy just couldn't see it.

When he looked at Julie, he saw a snooty, self-absorbed girl who was full of herself. And because of that, he didn't really care to invest much effort into getting to know her. He was content to keep her at arm's length and maintain a superficial, yet polite relationship, just to avoid any awkwardness.

But then one day, through a strange set of circumstances, the awkwardness caught up to Andy in the worst possible way.

Andy and Julie both attended a university three hours away from home. One weekend, when Andy was planning to drive home, Julie's mom asked her to come home as well. But Julie, who didn't have a car, told her mom that she didn't feel comfortable taking the bus that late on a Friday night. So Julie's mom—never one to give up easily—called Andy's mom, and the two of them made arrangements for Julie to ride back with Andy.

"Oh, that's just great!" Andy thought sarcastically to himself when he heard the news. *"Three painful hours with Julie! What could be worse?!"*

He then spent the next several days unsuccessfully trying to figure out a way out of this uncomfortable situation—considering everything from faking an injury to pretending there was a death in the family!

The weekend finally came. Andy arrived at Julie's apartment building, and she came down to meet him. They made small talk for about 15 minutes in the car, but Andy didn't know if he could keep this up for another two hours and 45 minutes. This ride was going to be painful!

Then suddenly—out of the blue—Julie said, *"Andy, there's something I've wanted to tell you for a long time, but just haven't had the chance. Can we talk about it now?"*

"Oh great! Here we go," Andy thought to himself. *"As if it weren't awkward enough already! Now Miss Fancy Pants over here wants to have a serious conversation. Who does she think she is?"*

"You know, Andy," Julie continued, *"I don't know why I feel this way, and I'm sure it's just in my head, but I've always felt intimidated around you."*

Andy's jaw dropped.

"I mean, I think you're a great guy. You seem so friendly and outgoing most of the time, but somehow that changes when I'm around. I feel like you hate being around me, and I get really nervous around you because of that. I know it's probably all in my head, right?" Julie asked.

Needless to say, that isn't what Andy was expecting! It turned out that Julie had misread Andy just as much as Andy had misread Julie—a classic example of perception being stronger than reality.

Andy didn't really know Julie—he thought he did, but he didn't. It was his perception of her that controlled his willingness to spend time with her and get to know her. But thanks to an assist from his mom, Andy got to know the real Julie that day. And Julie got to know the real Andy.

And the two have now been happily married for over 25 years.

CHAPTER 7

OUR FATHER IN HEAVEN

*A*ndy and Julie are a great example of what happens when reality confronts perception. It would've been a real shame if they'd never had that conversation that day. This great marriage *ALMOST* didn't happen due to their incorrect perceptions of each other. They each *thought* they knew the other person, but they didn't. Once they got to know the truth about each other, they fell in love.

But where would they be now had that conversation not taken place? Andy would still be convinced that Julie is stuck up *(even though she isn't)*, and Julie would be certain that Andy hated being around her *(which isn't true either)*. Each one would still be operating out of a misperception about the other, and that misperception would have stopped them from ever having an intimate relationship. Now, let's shift gears . . .

What do you see when you look at God? What do you think He sees when He looks at you?

I've found that every single person on this planet has an image of God in their head. You might not be able to articulate that image, but it's there. You may have inherited that image from your parents, or from your church, or from a movie, but it's there. And it will affect your life in more ways than you realize.

In fact, just as it did with Andy and Julie, your perception of God will have an even greater impact on your life than the reality of who He really is.

For example, some people have an image of God as an angry tyrant, someone who sits up in heaven and shouts out orders to His creation on earth.

"THOU SHALT NOT DO THIS" and *"THOU SHALT NOT DO THAT!* And *"If thou decidest to breaketh minest commandments, thou shalt be destroyed!"*

Would this image affect your ability to relate to God?

Of course, it would!

If this is your image, you are doing just about anything to avoid God. I mean, who wants to hang out with Hitler? You are walking on eggshells around Him and doing your best to avoid falling into what you think are the "major" sins.

And because your image of God is that of a tyrant, you likely aren't asking God for help. Why? Because your God is a tyrant . . . a dictator . . . someone who doesn't care about you, and therefore doesn't want to help you.

If that's your image of God, what do you think your response would be if you heard about a weekend retreat at your local church? *"Come spend a whole weekend—just you and God one-on-one for three whole days!"*

NO THANK YOU!

Perception trumps reality. Your perception of who God is impacts you more than the reality of who He is.

Another group of people might have a complete opposite view of God. To them, He isn't angry at all—He never gets angry! To them, God is "laid back," "easygoing," and an all-around "cool guy in the sky."

"Hey, little earth buddy, this is God calling from heaven. I want you to do your best to avoid some of that "bad" stuff down there, if you can. But if you can't, don't sweat it too much. I wouldn't want to mess up your schedule for the rest of the weekend—I know you've got a good one planned! See you on Sunday . . . or whenever you're not too busy!"

If this is your view of God, you probably don't take your spiritual life very seriously. This is like the kid in college who knows he's going to get a job at his parents' company after he finishes school. He doesn't care what grades he gets. He just needs to avoid failing, and if he does, he's good to go. So he parties all during college and does just enough to squeak by.

You also probably aren't trying very hard in your spiritual life. You're going through life thinking that God is your servant, here to please you and give you what you want—and not vice versa. You'll nonchalantly ignore any verses or messages that speak "resisting evil" or "striving to bloodshed" against sin. *"What's the big deal? After all, God is cool, right? He's all about love, isn't He?"*

Once again, perception trumps reality.

Some people see God as neither angry nor happy. Instead they see Him as cold and callous, someone who's just there to keep the universe afloat and make sure the planets don't collide. He isn't emotionally involved in our lives because He's busy. And that's understandable; I mean, He is in charge of managing the entire universe!

"Hello, Mr. and Mrs. Johnson. Thank you for being here today. We have a busy agenda, so let's get started right away. I need you to get your lives in order. You need to start reading

the Bible at least once per day, help at least one old lady cross the street per week, and be sure to give 10% of your income on a biweekly basis—and that's before taxes, not after! Thank you and have a nice day."

If this is your view of God, then you're more focused on the rules of religion vs. having a relationship with God. In fact, the whole concept of a "relationship with God" is difficult for you to comprehend. I mean, if God is nothing more than your boss, why would you want to have a relationship with Him? Who looks forward to growing a deeper relationship with their boss?

The person who has this view of God is probably a good person, who usually does the right things, but never really experiences the depth and intimacy that a relationship with God is supposed to have. They would just be going through the motions.

In case you haven't gotten the point yet, perception trumps reality. Like Andy and Julie, you might be living with a misperception about who God is and why He does what He does. And that perception affects you in ways you can't see. It affects both your ability and your desire to relate to your Creator.

We need to take the same approach that Julie took when she got into the car with Andy. We need to confront God directly. We need to tell Him what we're thinking and how we're feeling, and give Him a chance to respond. It's time to find out the truth about God.

Are you ready to get into the car and meet the real God?

THINKING OUTSIDE THE CAVE

Imagine for a moment that you live in a cave. You sleep in a cave, you eat in a cave, you do everything in a cave. All you've ever known is life in a cave.

And then one day, you hear a knock at your cave door. It's a man in a suit with a crew of cameramen behind him. He's the host of a hot new reality show called "Extreme Cave Makeover," and he's offering you $10 million to make whatever kind of improvements you'd like to your cave.

Did you hear that? Ten million dollars to spend on improving your cave any way you'd like. What do you think you'd say?

"Wow! That's really great! I'd love to make some improvements around here. Would it be possible to make the window in the corner a little bit bigger? It gets kinda stuffy in here when the whole family comes to visit, especially on burrito night. But a larger window would really make a difference. And if you could even add a second window, that would be fantastic!

"Also, my neck has really been bothering me lately, and I think it's from sleeping on these rocks all night. Do you think we could make some grass grow in here so I could sleep on that instead? That would be super!

"And, while we're at it, let's splurge! Let's paint the walls purple and the ceiling green, and let's have some fun with it!

"Do you think we could do all that, sir?"

ARE YOU KIDDING ME? That's all you'd want? Purple walls? Grass to sleep on? An extra window for burrito night?

Come on, man, be more creative! Think outside the cave a little! There's a whole world out there that you're missing out on. Don't ask for grass, ASK FOR CARPET! Or even better, ASK FOR A BED! And don't ask for a window, ASK FOR

WALLS—get four of them and you'll have something called a ROOM! You'll like it if you just give it a try.

THERE'S SO MUCH MORE OUT THERE THAT YOU DON'T REALIZE!

If you were that caveman, you would have missed out on a great opportunity—the chance of a lifetime. Why is that? Why did you settle for so little? Why didn't you ask for more?

Simple. Because you didn't know that was an option; you weren't able to think outside the cave. You don't know about houses or condos or beachfront properties. You only know one thing: caves. So, when you were asked what you wanted, you responded logically: *"I have a good cave. Now, how can I make it a better cave?"*

That's exactly what we do with God.

HE IS NOT LIKE US

We don't know what God looks like. We don't know what He sounds like. We don't know how He thinks or how He feels towards certain things.

(Of course, Bible-believing Christians will be quick to point out that we can learn all those things from the Scriptures. I agree 100%. However, most of us form our image of God well before we begin reading the Bible. And often, it's our incorrect image of God that clouds our reading of His Word, and prohibits us from being able to accept its authority in our lives. So go with me on this one.)

We don't know God because we are not God. We are human beings—always have been and always will be. We don't know what it's like to be God, but instead of humbling ourselves and admitting that we have no idea what God looks like, we try to explain Him in a way that fits with what we do know. We make God into someone who's like us, but just a little better.

It might work for a little but not for long:

- *"I am a nice person; therefore, God must be a really nice person."*
- *"I get sad when I see people mistreated, so God must get really sad when He sees people mistreated."*
- *"I like my children (most of the time), so God must like His children all of the time."*

So far, so good. But what happens when we go a little deeper:

- *"I hold grudges when someone lies to me or lets me down in some way, so, I guess God must hold grudges too." (WRONG)*
- *"I would never allow something bad to happen to my child if it was in my power to stop it, so I guess God would stop all the bad stuff if He could too." (VERY WRONG)*
- *"I am willing to give people a second chance, and a third chance, and maybe even a fourth or fifth chance, but at some point, you run out of chances. I guess God has more chances to offer, but you can probably run out with Him too." (VERY, VERY, VERY WRONG)*

See the problem here? God isn't like us. He isn't anything close to us. He isn't just some superhuman, super nice, Gandhi-on-steroids. He's completely different from us. HE'S GOD!

Listen to what God says through the prophet Isaiah:

"For My thoughts are not your thoughts, nor are your ways My ways," says the Lord. "For as the heavens are higher than the earth, so are My ways higher than your ways, and My thoughts than your thoughts." (Isaiah 55:8-9)

Did you catch that? God says, *"With all due respect, dear human, you are NOT like me. Or rather, I am not like you. I am different . . . way different. My thoughts are not like your thoughts. My ways are not like your ways. I don't think like you, I don't act like you, I don't hold grudges like you . . . I AM NOT LIKE YOU!"*

In fact, because God knows that we like numbers, He's quantified the distance between us and Him. He says, "As the heavens are higher than the earth." That's the distance between us and God.

How far is that? Let's run the numbers.

Forget about "the heavens" for a minute and let's just stick with our own solar system. The "heavens" implies the furthest point in the created world, but let's start a little closer to home. Let's start with the Sun. How far is the Sun from the Earth?

The answer? Approximately 93 million miles (give or take a half million miles). Do you know how far 93 million miles is?

Once you get into such large distances, scientists stop measuring in miles and start using light years—the distance that light travels in one year moving at (surprise, surprise) the speed of light. So at the speed of light—approximately 186,000 miles per second (not per hour or per minute, but PER SECOND)—a ray of light leaving the Sun takes roughly eight minutes to travel 93 million miles and hit the Earth.

Eight minutes!!!! Are you kidding me? You turn on a spotlight atop the Empire State Building, and within seconds, the whole city can see it. But if you turn on a slightly brighter light called THE SUN, you'd have to count to almost 500 before seeing it down here on Earth? That's crazy!

> "As the heavens are higher than the earth, so are My ways higher than your ways, and My thoughts than your thoughts." (Isaiah 55:9)

And that's just the Sun. Let's go further. Let's take a look at one of the planets in our solar system—every fifth grade boy's favorite planet: URANUS!

How far is Uranus above the Earth?

Because the solar system is in constant motion, the distance between Earth and Uranus changes daily. At its closest, it is 1.6 billion miles, and at its furthest, it is 1.98 billion miles. Let's go with the smaller number to be conservative.

How far is 1.6 billion miles?

We just saw that a ray of light from the Sun takes 8 minutes to travel 93 million miles and hit the Earth. At 1.6 billion miles, a ray of light leaving Uranus would take roughly 143 minutes to get here! That's close to two and a half hours traveling at the speed of light!!!

> "As the heavens are higher than the earth, so are My ways higher than your ways, and My thoughts than your thoughts." (Isaiah 55:9)

And that's just Uranus; that's still in our solar system. We haven't even gotten to the thousands of other galaxies that astronomers have discovered outside of our own, such as Galaxy MACS0647-JD, which was discovered to be 13.3 billion light years away!

Not 13.3 billion miles . . . 13.3 billion LIGHT YEARS! How far is that?

- Light traveling from Sun to Earth: 8 minutes
- Light traveling from Uranus to Earth: 2.5 hours
- Light travelling from MACS0647-JD to Earth: 13.3 billion light years

And God says all that is still less than the distance between Him and us . . . WOW!

BY REVELATION, NOT BY REASONING

The truth of the matter is we cannot know God unless He reveals Himself to us. God is too big for us to simply "figure out." Thinking harder won't get us anywhere—He's God. He can only be known as He chooses to reveal Himself.

Jesus said it this way:

> "Nor does anyone know the Father except the Son,
> and the one to whom the Son wills to reveal Him."
> (Matthew 11:27)

That isn't to say that we don't have a part to play in the process, by asking questions and trying to learn all we can about God (and reading wonderful books like this, of course!). But without God revealing Himself to us, we aren't going to get very far.

That's why I love that account of the two blind men written by the Evangelist Matthew in chapter 20 of his Gospel.

> Two blind men sitting by the road, when they heard that Jesus was passing by, cried out, saying, "Have

> mercy on us, O Lord, Son of David!" Then the mul-
> titude warned them that they should be quiet; but
> they cried out all the more, saying, "Have mercy
> on us, O Lord, Son of David!" (Matthew 20:30-31)

These guys may have been blind, but they certainly weren't dumb.

They were smart enough to know that they couldn't make themselves see; they couldn't wish their way to vision. They couldn't just try really, really hard to solve their blindness. Even if they read every book about eyes, and listened to every lecture about vision, and spent all their money on the finest glasses that the Hollywood stars wear . . .

. . . THEY WOULD STILL BE BLIND!

There wasn't anything they could do to get their vision. It wasn't a matter of time or effort or money. They needed help.

> So Jesus stood still and called them, and said, "What
> do you want Me to do for you?" They said to Him,
> "Lord, that our eyes may be opened." So Jesus had
> compassion and touched their eyes. And immedi-
> ately their eyes received sight, and they followed
> Him. (Matthew 20:32-34)

Did you see that? They realized they were blind . . . they found Jesus . . . they asked for help to be able to see . . . AND THEIR EYES RECEIVED SIGHT.

I love that story!

That's the only way we can see God. We can't figure Him out. He's Infinite—boundless, outside the limits of time and space. He's Immutable—unchanging, the same today as He was 10,000 years ago, and will be forever. And He's absolutely

Incomprehensible—way too far above what our minds can understand or comprehend or "figure out."

That's why the only solution here is to ask God to reveal Himself to you. You'll never know Him otherwise.

I love how those blind men did it. They could have pretended they were fine, or that they didn't need help. They could have put on the *"no, don't worry about me, I'm okay"* act. They could have accepted their blindness and settled for a subpar life, a life where they would never know what they were missing out on. But they didn't. They cried out for help: *"Lord, that our eyes may be opened."*

That is my prayer, and I hope it's yours too. If so, go ahead and close your eyes now (just like the blind men) and prove it. Say that prayer: *"Lord, that my eyes may be opened."*

Ask God to open your eyes and help you see Him . . . the real Him—not the image that your parents gave you, or that you've lived with your whole life. Ask God to open your eyes and allow you to see Him as He truly is.

First thing you'll see? GOD IS GOOD.

CHAPTER 8

HE IS A GOOD FATHER

*A*nother homicide report on the nightly news. Another serial sex offender on the loose. Another drunk driving accident claims the life of an innocent victim who just happened to be in the wrong place at the wrong time. Another gunman walks into an elementary school and does the unthinkable—not only taking the lives of several children, but robbing many more of their innocence and their right to just be kids.

All those events leave you and me asking the same question: *WHERE IS GOD?*

How come He doesn't do anything? Why does He just let this stuff happen? Doesn't He have the power to stop it? How come He's just sitting back when all this bad stuff is happening? Could it be that He's UNABLE to do anything about it? Or maybe, He just doesn't WANT to do anything? Why wouldn't God stop this?

If you've ever struggled with questions like these, then trust me, you're not alone. In my experience, this is the #1 question people have about God, and therefore it becomes the #1 ROADBLOCK between us and an authentic relationship with our Father in heaven. So, let's dig a little deeper into this question and see where it's really coming from.

Who are we really concerned about? The children dying in Africa? The victims of sex trafficking in the Philippines? The children forced into labor in China? As much as we may try to convince ourselves that our concern is for others who are being treated unfairly, the victims we care most about are the ones who are reading this book right now . . . OURSELVES!

Why would God give ME a father who would treat me that way?

Why wouldn't God heal MY mother when she was sick and I prayed so hard?

How come God can't help ME find a job that lasts?

How come no matter what I do, I still can't find a decent guy who's interested in ME?

The real question we're asking is this: *Is God working with me or against me? Is He on my side or not? I believe that He is all-powerful and that He holds the world in His hands, but then why doesn't He use that power to help ME and make MY LIFE any better? Why does He leave me to suffer like this when He has the power to snap His fingers and fix it all?*

Why, God, why?

These questions may not be *easy*, but I believe the answer is *simple*. They can all be answered by one single phrase — three simple words that have the power to transform your mind and your attitude, and thereby transform your life as well.

The magical phrase? GOD IS GOOD.

Yep, that's it. Those three words can change your life in ways you've never imagined.

And you're about to get a crash course in how.

57

IS HE A GOOD GUY OR NOT?

From a young age, we've always known that the world is divided into two groups: good guys and bad guys. That's just how it is. Good guys do everything they can to protect the innocent and defend those who can't defend themselves. Good guys fight for justice and put bad guys in their place. And most importantly, good guys always find a way to save the damsel in distress—usually without breaking a sweat or messing up their hair in the process.

Those are the "good guy" rules. They CANNOT be broken. If you don't abide by those rules, or if you choose not to follow them, you lose your "good guy" status. In other words, if Spiderman just sits back and does nothing as the Green Goblin tries to run a train full of people into the Hudson River, then he is no longer a good guy! He just lost his "good guy" membership card.

Sorry, but those are the rules.

But what happens when God doesn't follow those rules? What happens when bad stuff happens and God doesn't do anything about it? When He just watches it all happen? This is especially troublesome if you believe that God is Almighty and that He *COULD* step in at any moment . . . but He doesn't.

Said another way: Is God GOOD or not?

I know it seems like a no-brainer here, but humor me. Is God "good" or not? What do you honestly believe? We know what the answer is supposed to be, but is that how we really feel?

I guess the starting point would be to define what we mean by "good." What does "good" mean anyway? It's one of those words that we all understand and know intuitively, but isn't so easy to define. How would you define "good"?

Going to the dictionary may help, but my guess is that it'll just confuse you more. One dictionary has 58 definitions for "good." Let me repeat . . . 58 DEFINITIONS! What does it mean when you need 58 ways to define one word? It means that even Merriam-Webster doesn't know what it means!

But not being able to *define* "good" doesn't stop us from thinking we can *identify* it when we see it. We all have an idea about what's "good" and what's "not good."

- It's "good" when I get a raise.
- It's "good" when the pain in my lower back goes away.
- It's "good" when that boy asks me out.
- It's "good" when my team wins the big game.
- It's "good" when my in-laws move to Alaska.
- It's "good" when my boss gets a hernia and has to quit, and I get his job and his office and his parking spot.

Uh . . . wait a minute . . . are you sure all of those things are "good"? Do you think everyone else would agree? Would your boss and your in-laws agree? How about the fans of the other team that didn't win that game? And you said that it would be "good" if that boy asks you out, but would the other single girls also agree?

Could it be that our definition of "good" isn't as objective as we think? Could it be that our idea of what's "good" vs. "not good" has less to do with making the world a better place and more to do with just making us happy at the moment? Can one person's "good" be another person's "not good"?

Houston, we have a problem.

(RE)DEFINING GOODNESS

It's clear that our definition of "good" needs some work. It's not as absolute as we thought. In fact, there are three problems with the way we usually define "goodness."

Our definition is SUBJECTIVE.

It differs from person to person. Your idea of "good" isn't the same as someone else's; it's specific to you. For you, it's "good" when you get the promotion, but for your coworker who was vying for the same position, it is "not good."

For you, it's "good" when it turns out that your car doesn't need that $600 repair, but for your mechanic, who needs to find a way to pay for his daughter's braces, it is "not good."

For you, it's "good" when you put 75 cents in the vending machine and wind up getting two Twinkies instead of one. But for the guy who was there before you, who also paid 75 cents, but the Twinkie got stuck on the way down, it is "not good". . . very, very "not good."

Our definition of "good" is subjective.

Our definition is SHORTSIGHTED.

Raise your hands if you've ever wanted something really really badly, and begged God for it in prayer because you just knew that it would be the best thing ever . . . and then you later got it, and regretted the day you ever asked for it.

Has that ever happened to you? Be honest.

Or the opposite—raise your hand if you've ever really really NOT wanted something and prayed for God to remove it from your life, and He didn't . . . and then you later thanked God for it, and realized it was actually a source of blessing in your life.

Anyone want to raise both hands on that one?

Our definition of "goodness" is extremely shortsighted; it fluctuates over time. The things we once may have thought were "good," we later realize are actually "not good." Like that dream house that you always dreamed about . . . the same one that put you so far in debt that you still haven't recovered. Or that new job that you were just *DYING* for . . . the same one that caused you to work 80 hours per week and lose your family. We don't always know what's good for us.

And vice versa—we don't always know what's NOT good for us either. The very things we once hoped God would remove from our lives, we later come to see are blessings in disguise. Like that illness that ended up being the reason you reconciled with your sister, or that "hitting rock bottom" that became the impetus for you to finally get your life in order.

Our definition of "good" is terribly shortsighted.

Our definition is SELF-SERVING.

This one's a no-brainer. No matter what you say or how much you try to convince yourself otherwise, the truth is this: Your definition of "good" focuses only on what's "good" for YOU!

It isn't about world peace as much as it's about MY peace and MY safety when I travel. It isn't about finding a cure for a global disease as much as it's about finding a cure for MY sick mother. It isn't about being fair to the workforce; it's about being fair to ME!

Maybe we aren't quite the "goodness" experts we thought we were after all!

Our idea of "goodness" is subjective, shortsighted and highly self-serving. It's time to come up with a new definition—a better standard for measuring "goodness." We need something more solid . . . more objective . . . more absolute.

ABSOLUTE GOODNESS

"No one is good but One, that is, God." (Mark 10:18)

We have two options when it comes to figuring out whether God is "good" or "not good." We can make up our own definition *(which we saw would be subjective, shortsighted and self-serving)* and judge God's actions against that definition. Or we can believe that God *IS* good, and judge our own definition against what He does.

The question is who gets to define what "good" is? Do I set the standard, and then God has to meet it? Or is God the standard, and then I change my definition accordingly? Do I tell God when something is "good," or does He tell me? Who defines "good"?

There are only two options here: Either your definition will judge God's actions (this job is "good," and therefore God is "not good" because He didn't allow me to get it), or His actions will determine your definition (God is "good" and He didn't allow me to get the job, so therefore the job must be "not good" for me).

Do you see the difference? The choice is yours.

This dilemma isn't anything new to humanity. If you go back to the story of the first human beings on the planet—Adam and Eve—you'll see that they struggled with the same issue. They believed they should set the standard of what's good and what's not good. They didn't trust God's definition, and that got them into a tiny bit of trouble.

We'll pick up their story in Genesis 3. At this time in history, life was pretty groovy for Adam and Eve; there wasn't really too much to complain about. The weather was nice. They had plenty of pets. There was never any traffic. They never had to wait in line at the DMV. I'd say life was pretty "good" for Adam and Eve.

In fact, when God made the world, He paused several times to declare just how "good" things were. The phrase *"and God saw that it was good"* is repeated several times throughout Genesis 1. And it actually got even more "good" after the final day of creation when *"God saw everything that He had made, and indeed it was VERY GOOD." (Genesis 1:31).*

Wow! Very good! From God's own mouth? I mean, if God says life is good . . . actually, VERY GOOD . . . who are we to complain? Adam and Eve had it made!

Or so it seemed.

You know the story, so I'll spare you the details. A serpent comes along one day and starts talking to Eve about a piece of fruit. He says, "Hey, Eve, look at this. Wanna try? Come on, you know you want to. Everybody's doing it. It'll make you feel real good." *(That's the "1980s' Afterschool Special" paraphrase of Genesis 3:1-4.)*

Eve knows she shouldn't eat that fruit, but she's having a tough time convincing herself why. *"Is it really that big a deal? Why would God want to deny me this pleasure? Why does He get to determine what's good for me and what isn't?"*

Finally, the serpent convinces her with one statement:

> "For God knows that in the day you eat of it your eyes will be opened, and you will be like God, knowing GOOD and evil." (Genesis 3:5)

Boom! He got her! He found the weak spot. He said if you eat this fruit, then *YOU* can decide what's good and not good. And that was all she wrote . . .

> So when the woman saw that the tree was GOOD
> for food, that it was pleasant to the eyes, and a tree
> desirable to make one wise, she took of its fruit and
> ate. She also gave to her husband with her, and he
> ate. (Genesis 3:6)

Up to this point, God had been the One setting the standard on what was "good" and "not good." He told them it would be good for them to "be fruitful and multiply," and it would be good for them to "have dominion over every living thing that moves on the earth." He also told them that it would be "not good" for them to be alone. God defined "good," and they accepted it and judged life by that standard.

They probably didn't understand everything God was telling them or why things had to be a certain way, but they knew enough to trust Him and accept His standard. And as long as they trusted God and lived by His standards, life really was "good"—actually "VERY GOOD." They were reaping the rewards of God's goodness without even realizing it.

So what happened in Genesis 3:6? The greatest tragedy in the history of mankind. Adam and Eve stopped trusting in God's goodness and instead decided that they knew better. *THEY* were now writing the rules; *THEY* were determining what was "good" and "not good." *THEY* would now set the definition of goodness, and if God didn't meet it, that meant actually *HE* wasn't good.

Sound familiar?

The fall of mankind can be traced back to one horrible, tragic, and catastrophic decision: the decision to doubt God's goodness.

And we've been making the same mistake ever since.

TRUST THE BAKER, NOT THE INGREDIENTS

My wife makes the best chocolate chip pancakes in the world! It's a Saturday morning tradition around our house—no matter how early everyone wakes up, we all wait for Mom to make her world-famous pancakes for breakfast. And sometimes when the kids are really hungry, they expedite the waking-up process by *"accidentally"* walking into our room and jumping on our bed.
THEY WANT THEIR PANCAKES!

Do you know what goes into a chocolate chip pancake? The actual ingredients? Every week I see my wife put several not-so-tasty items into a bowl, mix it all up, and then POOF! Out comes the world's greatest chocolate chip pancakes—each bite dripping with sweet, chocolatey love!

But what goes into that bowl? Some flour, a cup or two of milk, a few eggs, a stick of butter, some baking powder, a little sugar wouldn't hurt, and of course . . . the main ingredient . . . plenty of CHOCOLATE CHIPS!

So every time I eat a bite of those pancakes, what I'm really eating is a little bit of each of those ingredients: flour, milk, eggs, butter, baking powder, sugar, and chocolate chips. I may not pay attention to any of them except the chocolate chips, but they're all in there. They're all *WORKING TOGETHER* to make the final product so tasty.

But let's say I didn't want to wait for Marianne to make the pancakes; I'm in a rush and want to cut out the middle man. So I gather all the ingredients together, but then skip the mixing and cooking steps. *(Who's got time for that?)* Instead I take each ingredient and consume it independently.

I start with a spoonful of flour . . . and then I drink a half cup of milk . . . and then take a bite out of that stick of butter,

65

followed by a raw egg or two. And then a spoon of sugar, a spoon of baking powder, and the highlight of the recipe, a handful of chocolate chips!

Mmmmmmm. . . . appetizing, isn't it? Probably not.

Isn't it strange that when you eat those items individually, they don't taste very good? But somehow, when you mix them all *together* and cook them in a frying pan, they seem to taste a whole lot better! Strange, isn't it?

> And we know that all things work together for good to those who love God, to those who are the called according to His purpose. (Romans 8:28)

Your life is a lot like that mixing bowl. God adds a variety of things into it, different ingredients that He's using to make the masterpiece called "Your Life." He'll put some things in that you love and that'll make you say, *"Give me MORE of those"* (like the sugar, milk, and chocolate chips). But He'll also put some things in that you *don't* particularly care for, things that might not taste very good on their own, but you need them to make the recipe complete (like the baking powder and the raw eggs).

But God knows what He's doing. He has a plan. He knows what you need . . . EXACTLY what you need. He isn't guessing or making it up as He goes along. You may not like all the ingredients, but ultimately, you'll discover that they're all there for a reason. They're all working together "for good." The chef doesn't promise that every ingredient will be good on its own, but rather that the final product—*after all the ingredients have been allowed to work together*—will be good. God is no different. Can you trust that? Can you trust that God is "good" and that His plan is "good"? Can you trust that, like my wife with her chocolate chip pancakes, God specializes in creating great-ness out of unlikely ingredients? Can you trust that He indeed makes *"all things WORK TOGETHER for good to those who love God"?*

You may not get the job you want . . . or that relationship may not turn out how you hoped . . . or the diagnosis may not be what you wanted to hear . . . but can you still trust that God is working all things together for good? Taking all the different ingredients and mixing them together in such a way to make "good" in your life?

Don't make the same mistake that Adam and Eve made. They stopped trusting in God's goodness and began trusting in their own. That one mistake cost them everything. When they trusted His goodness, they reaped all the benefits of it. But that all ended once they thought they knew better.

> Then the Lord God said, "Behold, the man has become like one of Us, to know good and evil . . . therefore the Lord God sent him out of the garden of Eden to till the ground from which he was taken." (Genesis 3:22-23)

The only way for me to reap the goodness of Marianne's pancakes is to trust her. I must trust that she knows what she's doing, and that she knows what's best for me. I may be tempted, though, to look at the ingredients and reject some of them, thinking that I know best.

No! I don't want the eggs in there. I don't like raw eggs. I ate a raw egg last week and it made me throw up. NO RAW EGGS! Just put in more chocolate chips instead.

But doing so only hurts one person . . . ME!

FR. ANTHONY MESSEH

The same holds true with God. At times, we're tempted to feel like we are the master chef, and this is God's first day on the job. *"Give us more of this, God . . . and less of that. Take this out, and don't let me taste this again. I only want that other thing over there. Give me more and more of that. That's what you'd do if You truly cared about me."*

God is good, not us. He's the master chef, not us. He's the One with the recipe for success, not us.

The only way to reap the benefits of being married to the world's greatest chocolate chip pancake maker is to put my trust not in the ingredients, but in the one mixing them together. Similarly, the only way to reap the benefits of being a child of God is to put my trust not in the circumstances of my life, but in the One who is working all things together for good to those who love Him.

Are you ready to trust God? Are you ready to believe in His goodness over your own?

If so, get ready to taste the goodness.

"Oh, taste and see that the Lord is good;
blessed is the man who trusts in Him!" (Psalm 34:8)

CHAPTER 9

HE IS A GRACIOUS FATHER

O ne of my all-time favorite stories in the Bible also happens to be one of the most well-known. It's commonly referred to as "The Feeding of the Five Thousand":

> And the apostles, when they had returned, told Him [Jesus] all that they had done. Then He took them and went aside privately into a deserted place belonging to the city called Bethsaida. But when the multitudes knew it, they followed Him; and He received them and spoke to them about the kingdom of God, and healed those who had need of healing. When the day began to wear away, the twelve came and said to Him, "Send the multitude away, that they may go into the surrounding towns and country, and lodge and get provisions; for we are in a deserted place here."
>
> But He said to them, "You give them something to eat." And they said, "We have no more than five loaves and two fish, unless we go and buy food for all these people." For there were about five thousand men.

Then He said to His disciples, "Make them sit down in groups of fifty." And they did so, and made them all sit down.

Then He took the five loaves and the two fish, and looking up to heaven, He blessed and broke them, and gave them to the disciples to set before the multitude. So they all ate and were filled, and twelve baskets of the leftover fragments were taken up by them. (Luke 9:10-17)

I LOVE THIS STORY! It's always been one of my favorites. And every time I read it, I learn to appreciate it just a little bit more.

First of all, I LOVE fish sandwiches! In fact, I have an affinity for most fish food items: fish tacos, fish sticks, fish and chips, fish burgers, you name it! If it's breaded and fried, I'll take it! And of all the different options of fish out there, this is my absolute favorite of them all . . . FREE fish! Yep, Jesus was just giving them away to everyone who showed up at the party.

And wait . . . it gets better! Not only is Jesus giving away fish sandwiches—once again, FREE fish sandwiches—but apparently, it's buffet style as well. ALL YOU CAN EAT! The Bible says that *they all ate and were FILLED.* In fact, there was so much food that even after everyone filled up, they collected 12 baskets of leftovers! NOW THAT'S MY KIND OF PARTY!

So right off the bat, this story hits me in two of my soft spots: my tummy and my wallet!

But there's more to it. The story also teaches an important principle about the nature and character of God, a principle that is essential to knowing God and relating to Him at a deeper level. And that principle is this: God is not only good, He's also GRACIOUS.

What does "gracious" mean? Unfortunately, we've lost a little of the true meaning of that word. Today when you say that someone is "gracious," you're saying that he is kind . . . or polite . . . or courteous. If you invite me over to your house and offered me tea and fish sticks, for example, I might say, *"Thank you for your gracious hospitality."*

But that isn't the true meaning of the word. "Gracious" literally means "full of grace." It means someone known for the overwhelming grace that he displays towards others. And in its original meaning, the word "grace" means an undeserved gift, one given with nothing expected in return. So, a gracious person is one who is known for giving gifts—not for the sake of receiving anything in return, but for the sake of giving alone.

Back to our principle: God is not only good, He is GRACIOUS as well.

What does it mean when we say that God is gracious? Go back to the story of the five loaves and two fish. Read it again and answer this question: *Did the people need food?*

Think before you answer.

Did the people *NEED* food? I mean, did they REALLY need food? Did they really, really, really need it at that moment? I'm not asking if they WANTED food *("I'm hungry"),* I'm asking if they NEEDED food *("I'm going to die of starvation").*

Did the people NEED food? Yes or no?

NO! They didn't. If you look at the story, it doesn't say that they even ASKED for food. It was the apostles who brought up the whole food thing (probably because they were hungry). They're the ones who said, *"The people are hungry, Jesus. Tell them to leave so they can eat, and we can eat too!"*

So if the people didn't need food, and actually didn't even ask for food, why would Jesus go out of His way to give them food?

The answer? Because God is GRACIOUS.

MORE THAN WELFARE

"God doesn't give you what you WANT; He only gives you what you NEED," yelled the preacher from behind the pulpit.

If you've been to church for any significant amount of time, I'll bet you've heard that before. We preachers want people to know that God is not some kind of magical genie who grants our every wish. We don't submit our list of requests to God like we do to Santa Claus, and then wait for presents to appear under the tree. That isn't how God works, and we want to make sure we beat it into people's heads:

"God won't give you something unless He determines that you really, really need it. So if it's anything less than a 100% life-or-death need, then you shouldn't expect it from God. Just be happy that He's given you air to breathe and water to drink; anything more than that is a bonus, and God will only give it to you if you really need it. Now, please be generous as we pass around the offering plate."

While of course I agree that God doesn't give us everything we want (no responsible parent would), is this really how it works? He only gives us things that we really, really need and nothing more? If that's the case, then God isn't really a father; He's more like a government welfare agency or the unemployment office. You go in, wait in a long line, present your case as to why you need something, and then hope for the best as God makes His decision.

Is God a stingy welfare agency, or is He a gracious Father? Does God only give us what we need? Or are there times when He gives us *MORE* than what we need?

Go back to the story of the five loaves and two fish. The people DIDN'T need food. If they really needed to eat so badly, then how come no one asked for food? Or how come no one left the party to go home and eat? Or how come no one knocked down the little boy and stole his lunch box? Do you mean to tell me that there were 5,000 starving Middle Eastern men on that mountain, and that little boy and his lunch box escaped unscathed? No way!

And even if they did need food, did they really need *THIS MUCH* food? Did they each need to eat until they were so full that they could eat no more? If God were nothing more than a welfare agency, then the Bible would say *"and each one received exactly two-thirds of a cracker and one fish nugget. No more, no less. And whoever wanted more had to fill out an application and come back in two weeks to see if his request was accepted."*

But that's not God. God doesn't just give us what we NEED; He gives us *MORE* than we need! Way more! He doesn't stop at bare minimum; He goes above and beyond! Why? Because God is not the Social Security office or the Department of Unemployment—God is a father . . . He's OUR father . . . and He's a gracious father. And a gracious father *ENJOYS* giving gifts to His children.

No one would have said that Jesus was negligent if He didn't feed the multitudes that day. In fact, Jesus had already given them what they really needed. The Bible says, *"He received them and spoke to them about the kingdom of God, and healed those who had need of healing."* He received them.

He spoke to them about the kingdom of God. He healed those who needed healing.

That's a pretty good day in my book. No one would argue if Jesus decided to call it quits after that. In fact, He could have said, *"I know you guys are tired and hungry. So therefore, I am wrapping up this service right now so that you can get home to eat and rest. Why? Because I love you and care about you."*

No one would have been upset; in fact, they probably would've clapped for Him. *(Wouldn't you clap if your pastor says the same thing this Sunday?)*

No one was expecting food. No one was waiting for food. No one even asked for food.

But Jesus insisted on giving them food. Why? Because He is gracious.

TAPPING INTO GOD'S GRACIOUSNESS

Umm . . . yeah, it's great that God is so giving and generous and desiring to give good gifts, but where is that graciousness in my life? How come I don't see any of it? All I see are desires left unmet . . . dreams left unfulfilled . . . and prayers left unanswered. How do I find God's graciousness in my life?

The key to unlocking God's graciousness is discussed just two chapters later, in Luke 11. Jesus is once again standing atop a mountain, but this time He isn't giving out sandwiches; He's teaching about prayer in His famous Sermon on the Mount.

> "So I say to you, ask, and it will be given to you; seek, and you will find; knock, and it will be opened to you. For everyone who asks receives, and he who seeks finds, and to him who knocks it will be opened.

If a son asks for bread from any father among you, will he give him a stone? Or if he asks for a fish, will he give him a serpent instead of a fish? Or if he asks for an egg, will he offer him a scorpion?

If you then, being evil, know how to give good gifts to your children, how much more will your heavenly Father give the Holy Spirit to those who ask Him!" (Luke 11:9-13)

The short answer is PRAYER. Prayer is what connects us to God's graciousness. Prayer is the passageway by which the good gifts of God come to us. Prayer is the means by which God works in us and in our lives. Prayer is the answer. Prayer, prayer, prayer!

But the answer doesn't lie in merely *SAYING* prayers. We all do that. We're experts in blurting out random prayers here and there—when we're afraid, or unsure, or in some kind of catastrophe. *"God, please help me,"* or *"God, give this to me,"* or *"God, please solve this problem."* We all say prayers. But that isn't what Jesus is talking about here. The question isn't do we *SAY* prayers, the question is do we *PERSIST* in prayer? There's a big difference.

Remember when we were kids and we used to do something called "ding-dong ditching"? Ding-dong ditching is when you ring someone's doorbell (ding-dong) and then run away (ditching). This would provide us . . . I mean . . . uh . . . THEM, you know, the kids who did this sort of thing . . . this would provide THEM hours and hours of entertainment on those long summer days.

I'm afraid that some of us are guilty of ding-dong ditching God in our prayers! We rattle off a random assortment of words: *"Bless me, help me, fix this, hurry up, thank you, You're the best, Amen!"* and then we run away as fast as we can. We go into prayer like we go into the dentist's office, thinking, *"This is going to be painful, so let's get in and get out of here as fast as we can."*

Is that the kind of prayer Jesus is talking about? Is that the prayer that leads to seeing the graciousness of God?

When Jesus says, *"Ask, and you will receive,"* the expression can more accurately be written, *"KEEP ASKING and you will receive."* Don't just ask and run (ding-dong ditch); KEEP asking and you will receive; KEEP seeking and you will find; KEEP knocking and the door will be opened to you.

God is a gracious father who delights in giving good gifts to His children, but we'll never see those gifts if we keep running away before He opens the door.

I'm not just talking about time in prayer—persistence is more than that. It's not a matter of *HOW LONG* your prayers are, it's a matter of *HOW SINCERE* they are. God asks, *"Are you just saying prayers to ease your conscience, or are you really desiring to communicate with Me? Are you just going through the motions of prayer because you think you're supposed to? Or am I a serious priority in your life?"*

Think back again to the story of the five thousand who were fed with five loaves and two fish. The people were out on that mountain, listening to Jesus, all day long. It was hot and they were tired, but they persisted and stayed out there ALL DAY LONG. As long as Jesus was on that mountain, they weren't going anywhere. They were going to persist for as long as He was there.

But imagine there is one young man who didn't persist. He came at the start, listened to a little bit of the teaching, and then decided to go home. He left before Jesus did the miracle and fed everyone.

And then if he is asked about Jesus, he might say, *"He's a nice guy, but I don't really know what the big deal is. He's not that much different than anybody else. In fact, I was surprised that He didn't really care that much about us. He didn't seem all that concerned that it was getting late and we were starting to get hungry. He just wanted to preach, preach, preach, and that was it."*

Would that be a fair assessment? Would it be fair to say that Jesus didn't care about feeding him? Or could it be that he wasn't that interested in sticking around to eat?

Persistence is the key to tapping into God's graciousness.

THE REWARDER OF THOSE WHO SEEK HIM

> He who comes to God must believe that He is, and that He is a rewarder of those who diligently seek Him. (Hebrews 11:6)

You'll never taste the graciousness of God in "ding-dong ditching" prayers. God is full of good gifts and He greatly desires to give those gifts to His children. That's what He meant when He said, *"If you then, being evil, know how to give good gifts to your children, how much more will your heavenly Father give the Holy Spirit to those who ask Him!"*

In other words, what Jesus is saying is this: *"If you, moms and dads, enjoy watching your kids open up presents on Christmas morning, then what makes you think I don't enjoy watching you open up My presents just as much? If you delight in helping your children fulfill their dreams, what makes you think I delight any less in helping you fulfill yours? If you know how to give gifts to your children—based on what's good for them, not just what they want—why can't you trust that I want to do the same for you?"*

As our Good Father and our Gracious Father, God has everything we need—not just the things that we ask for, but even the things that we don't ask for. But the means by which we will receive those gifts is directly related to the diligence we invest in seeking Him *(that's prayer)*.

In other words, it's your choice. You choose how much blessing God will pour into your life. You choose the amount of grace you will receive. He is a rich father, and He has many good gifts to give.

It's up to you how much you want in your life.

One final story to make my point clear. Imagine that a new ice cream store opens up near your house with tons of flavors and toppings to choose from. And in this store, there is a unique policy. You can have as much ice cream and as many toppings as you'd like—ALL FOR THE SAME PRICE. It doesn't matter if you take two scoops or 10 scoops; fruit toppings, no toppings, or the smashed-up fudge brownie toppings. It's all the same price, no matter how much you take.

The only caveat is that the store doesn't provide bowls, so you must bring your own. Whatever size bowl you bring will determine how much ice cream you walk away with. Bring a big bowl? Get lots of ice cream. Bring a small bowl? Get a lot less ice cream.

Those are the rules.

Let's say you and your friend both walk into the store. She brings a large one-gallon pitcher, but you only bring a four-ounce cup. She will walk out of there with one gallon of ice cream; you will have four ounces. Does that mean that the owner of the store loves her more than you? Does that mean that he is favoring her over you? Does that mean that he is not being fair to you?

Just like the owner of that ice cream store, God is a rewarder of those who diligently seek Him. He is rich in everything that we need in this life. Need wisdom? He's got it. Need patience? He's got that too. Need power or strength or guidance or healing??? You name it, He's got it! And because He is gracious, He loves to share it!

But the key will be you. How big is the bucket that you're bringing to God? How persistent and how diligent will you be in seeking Him?

Maybe now's a good time to find out. Put this book down for one minute and close your eyes and say a prayer. It doesn't need to be long; it just needs to be sincere. The issue isn't quantity, it's quality and sincerity of heart. Remember you're speaking to your Father, not the welfare office. You don't have to validate, justify, or prove anything. All you need to do is come with a sincere heart.

Your gracious Father is waiting and He's ready to go. Now's your chance.

Just be sure to bring a big bucket.

"And it will be that when he cries to Me, I will hear, for I am gracious." (Exodus 22:27)

CHAPTER 10

HE IS A NEAR FATHER

*A*s a priest, one question that I'm asked quite frequently is *"How can I change?"* Whether it's a bad habit, or a negative attitude, or a destructive thought pattern, we all have something that we wish we could change about ourselves.

Do you know what one factor influences your behavior more than any other? What one aspect of your life—if you could change it—has the ability to impact every other area?

It's not your education level or your family upbringing; it isn't your social class or economic status. Thankfully, it's something that is 100% within your power to change. Studies show that—aside from genetic predispositions—the #1 factor influencing your behavior is . . .

Your SELF-IMAGE. How you view yourself.

More than any other factor, your self-image is the rudder that steers the ship when it comes to the decisions you make and the behaviors you engage in. It is the autopilot of your life; no matter where you are, it guides you back to a certain set of behaviors which are in line with who your self-image says you are.

For example, imagine two first-year college students with similar upbringings and backgrounds, but with vastly different self-images. The first sees himself as a straight-A student, a valedictorian in waiting. The other sees himself as a below average student, lucky to just get into college in the first place.

Assume these two young men were in the same class and they got B's on their first exam. How would they each respond?

The first young man—the one who views himself as a straight-A student—would probably say, *"I guess I need to study a lot harder. I need to read more and party less. It won't be easy, but I need to find a way to get back on track as soon as possible."*

His self-image tells him that a B is unacceptable; it isn't in line with who he is.

The second student, on the other hand, the one who views himself as a below average student, would have a much different response. *"Woo-hoo! I got a B! This college stuff isn't going to be as hard as I thought. Thank God I did so well on that first exam. As long as I keep doing what I'm doing, I should be totally fine."*

His self-image tells him that a B is above what he's capable of, and therefore, he's perfectly content to maintain the status quo. He's already done better than he thought possible, so why put in any more effort?

Your self-image dictates your behavior. So, what do YOU see when you look in the mirror?

The husband who sees himself as a victim will behave accordingly—going passively through life, feeling helpless and unable to take control of his circumstances at work and at home. He's a victim, and he'll always be a victim until he starts believing that he's not.

The teenage girl who sees herself as nothing more than "a piece of trash" *(Forgive the expression, but that's, unfortunately, the phrase that I hear from many young people in describing themselves.)* will behave as such. She'll treat her body in such a way that devalues it, and she'll probably let others do the same.

Why? Not because she *IS* trash, but because she *THINKS* she's trash. She's allowed others to set her value. She's been told that she isn't worth very much—she's not smart enough, not pretty enough, not thin enough, and therefore not all that valuable.

And unfortunately, she believes it. And because she believes it, she behaves accordingly.

Once again, your self-image dictates your behavior.

Back in Chapter 7, I said that the two most important questions are *"What do you see when you look at God?"* and *"What do you think He sees when He looks at you?"*

We've been addressing the first question for the past two chapters: *"What do you see when you look at God."* We saw that God is good, and God is gracious. Now it's time to address the second question (which you can't properly answer until you've addressed the first; you must know who God is in order to know who you are).

Who am I in God's eyes? What does God see when He looks at me? How can I really know?

WHO'S THE LITTLE GUY UP IN THE TREE?

Enter Zacchaeus. You've heard of Zacchaeus before, haven't you? He's quite the famous man. He's so famous that they even wrote a song about him—ensuring that he'll never be forgotten, but rather immortalized and remembered in our hearts for years and years to come.

Zacchaeus was a wee little man,
And a wee little man was he.
He climbed up in a sycamore tree,
For the Lord he wanted to see.

Uhhh ... wait a minute ... that's not very nice. *"Zacchaeus was a wee little man and a wee little man was he?"* That's how the song starts? By calling him a *"wee little man"*? Does Zacchaeus know about those lyrics? Did he approve that first line? It doesn't exactly sound like how I'd like to be remembered in the history books.

But that's what Zacchaeus got—not Zacchaeus the wise, or Zacchaeus the humble, or Z-Man, or Z-Money *(my personal choice)*, or even just plain old Zack. Instead he wound up with *"Zacchaeus, the wee little man."*

With a nickname like that, it's no surprise then that Zacchaeus would struggle with his self-image. If children in Sunday schools all over the world are calling him *"a wee little man"* today, you can only imagine what they called him when he was growing up!

Zacchaeus didn't think very highly of himself *(pun intended)* and his poor self-image only grew worse as he grew older.

> Then Jesus entered and passed through Jericho. Now behold, there was a man named Zacchaeus who was a chief tax collector, and he was rich. And he sought to see who Jesus was, but could not because of the crowd, for he was of short stature. (Luke 19:1-3)

The first thing we learn about Zacchaeus is that he worked as a tax collector—actually, not just a tax collector, but the CHIEF tax collector. Back in the day, *"tax collector"* was synonymous with *"scum of the earth."* Tax collectors were the most hated people in Jewish culture. They were traitors who betrayed their own people for personal gain.

At that time, Israel was under the rule of the Roman Empire. And Rome required all Jewish citizens to pay taxes to Caesar. They collected those taxes through Jewish men known as tax collectors. They worked for Rome, aka, the bad guys.

And what made those tax collectors even more hated was that they would often inflate the tax rate and collect more than what was due. If you owed five pieces of silver, they'd tell you to pay six, and pocket the extra money themselves. *(That explains why the Bible said that Zacchaeus was rich.)* No one could argue with the tax collectors or put up a fight because they worked for Rome and were supported by the Roman military. The people had no choice but to pay.

SCUM OF THE EARTH INDEED!

That's what Zacchaeus was. That's *WHO* Zacchaeus was. He wasn't an honorable man. He wasn't a man of integrity. He was a liar and a cheat, a traitor and a thief. And on top of that, he was short! The Biblical account emphasizes that he *"was of short stature."*

Even the Bible is sticking it to this guy!

But the problem with Zacchaeus wasn't that he was bad (no one is inherently bad). The problem is that he *BELIEVED* he was bad; that's what he was always told, and he had no reason to believe otherwise.

So his behavior followed suit. He behaved like a bad guy is supposed to behave. He let his self-image be set by what others said and thought about him. That self-image then dictated his life.

But that's about to change. Jesus is in town. And Zacchaeus is about to meet Him. And when he does, everything changes. Jesus is about to show Zacchaeus who he *REALLY* is and what his true worth is in God's eyes.

And that changes everything.

YOU MAY BE FAR, BUT GOD IS STILL NEAR

> So he (Zacchaeus) ran ahead and climbed up into a sycamore tree to see Him, for He (Jesus) was going to pass that way. And when Jesus came to the place, He looked up and saw him, and said to him, "Zacchaeus, make haste and come down, for today I must stay at your house." So he made haste and came down, and received Him joyfully. (Luke 19:4-6)

Every time I read this story, I'm struck by the powerful lesson it teaches. It's a simple lesson, but one that has the power to change everything when we fully comprehend it. And that lesson, boys and girls, is this . . .

GOD IS NEAR.

That's right, God is near. He's near to you and He's near to me; He's near to each of us. There isn't one square inch in this universe that's beyond His reach. No matter where I am or where I go . . . no matter how many times I've strayed or how far I've gotten when I have strayed . . . regardless of how lost and distant I might feel today . . . the fact still remains . . . GOD IS NEAR!

The story of Zacchaeus proves it.

Here you have Jesus walking through a crowded street— hundreds of people all around, each fighting to get Jesus's attention, tugging at His robe, asking for a miracle. Yet somehow, in the midst of all that commotion, Jesus looks up and notices Zacchaeus—the little guy, way up there in that tall tree.

How did He even see him? How was He able to notice Zacchaeus up there, when there were so many people on the ground? It doesn't make sense. It would seem that Zacchaeus was too far away for Jesus to see him, or reach him, or even notice him. And even if He did notice him, He surely wouldn't want to talk to him, or even be seen greeting such a wicked tax collector . . . right?

Wrong! Zacchaeus was far, but God was still near to him.

Jesus spots Zacchaeus from a mile away and goes straight to him. As only Jesus can do, He finds a way to look past all the crowds and find the one guy who needed to be found this day—the one guy who felt so worthless and bad about himself that he was hiding in a tree because he was too embarrassed to let Jesus see him.

But Jesus found Zacchaeus. He found the guy who thought he was "too far" to be found. Jesus showed him that no matter how far he/anyone is, God is always near.

> "Zacchaeus, make haste and come down, for today I
> must stay at your house." (Luke 19:5)

Yep, that's right. The guy who was seen as the *"scum of the earth"*—both by others and by himself—is now hosting a dinner party with JESUS CHRIST HIMSELF as the guest of honor!

Not too shabby for that wee little man.

THE GOD WHO NOTICES

Have you ever felt forgotten by God? Have you ever felt like you've strayed too far to even be noticed by Him? Have you ever felt like God stopped caring about your problems or circumstances?

If so, take comfort in the story of Zacchaeus and know that God is near. He's always been near and He'll always be near. And because He's near, that means that GOD NOTICES YOU. You might not see it or feel it, but God is giving you His full attention every single minute of the day.

> "Are not five sparrows sold for two copper coins? And not one of them is forgotten before God. But the very hairs of your head are all numbered. Do not fear therefore; you are of more value than many sparrows." (Luke 12:6-7)

If you ever think that God has forgotten you, or that He's stop caring about your problems, go back and read that verse. If a tiny little sparrow—worth less than one-half of a copper coin *(the equivalent of somewhere between a quarter and a dime in modern U.S. currency)*—is never forgotten before God, then how could you think that you, His beloved child, would ever be forgotten?

Or if God cares about knowing the exact number of hairs on your head at this very moment *(for some of us, that's unfortunately not as challenging as it once was)*, then how can you think that He wouldn't care even more about whatever problems or circumstances you're going through?

Whether you realize it or not . . . whether you feel it or not . . . the truth is clear. God notices you and He notices everything about you. When you're sad, He sees it and is ready to pick you up. When you're happy, He sees it and is ready to rejoice with you. When you're confused, He sees it and is ready to guide you through whatever it is that life is throwing your way.

God is NEAR and He notices everything.

Having someone notice us and pay attention to us is one of our deepest human needs. Look at children. What happens to a child if he doesn't get attention? What do children do when they feel like no one is noticing them?

Some yell. Some throw stuff across the room. I once saw a child put a bucket on his head and bang his head on the floor to try to get his mom's attention. Kids will do anything to have someone pay attention to them.

But adults are different, right? We don't need attention like kids do . . . do we? Or maybe we're just a bit more sophisticated in how we express that need for attention.

We might not yell with our voices, but the way we dress ends up screaming much louder: *"LOOK AT ME! LOOK AT ME!"*

We may not go around throwing stuff, but we may instead go around BUYING stuff: a new watch, a new phone, a new car, a new house . . . anything to make us feel like we matter.

And I highly doubt that any of us are putting on buckets and hitting our heads on the floor (*if so, please close this book and seek help IMMEDIATELY*), but I'll bet we put on masks to hide our personalities, masks to hide who we *REALLY ARE*, and try to portray who we *WISH* we were.

We all want someone to pay attention to us, don't we?

The good news is that you don't need to do those things anymore. God sees you. God notices you. God pays close attention to every little detail of your life. You don't need to change anything about yourself to convince Him that you're important and worthy of His attention. He's already convinced!

In fact, not only does He never take His eyes off you, He goes even further. Look at how the prophet Isaiah describes it:

> But Zion said, "The Lord has forsaken me, and my Lord has forgotten me." Can a woman forget her nursing child, and not have compassion on the son of her womb? Surely they may forget, yet I will not forget you. See, I have inscribed you on the palms of My hands. (Isaiah 49:14-16)

WOW! God not only notices me and pays attention to me, but He takes it to another level when He says, *"I have inscribed you on the palms of My hands."* GOD HAS A TATTOO OF ME ON HIS HANDS! *(Not literally, of course, but figuratively; all tattoo haters, take a deep breath and relax, it's just a metaphor.)*

The world may tell you that you're nothing special . . . that there's nothing worth loving about you . . . that you've strayed too far and made too many mistakes. And you might even hear those words from your church or from religious people who specialize in the gift of discouragement and condemnation.

But whenever you hear those words, just remember that your face is tattooed on God's hands, and that tattoo will last forever. Every time He looks at His hands, He remembers you. You can never escape His care and His attention—even if you tried.

That makes you pretty special in my book.

HOW MUCH IS A CRUMPLED UP
$100 BILL WORTH?

A well-known speaker once began a lecture by holding a crisp $100 bill in front of his audience. He asked who in the audience would be interested in taking that bill if he were to offer it. Without hesitation, everyone raised their hand; no one thought twice.

He then crumpled the $100 bill into a messy, little wad. *"Who wants it now?"* he asked. Every hand was still raised.

Then he threw the wadded-up bill on the floor and began stomping it with his dirty boots. *"Who wants it now?"* he asked again. And again, every hand was still raised.

It's now been dirtied, beaten up, and stomped on . . . why would anyone still want it after all that?

Because it's still worth $100! No matter how dirty or beaten up it may be, it will always be worth exactly one hundred dollars. The value doesn't change just because the outside gets a little messy.

SAME WITH YOU!

Some of you can relate to the feeling of that $100 bill. You feel like you've messed up too badly . . . you've made too many mistakes . . . you'll never be able to get it right and get your life on track. You're just not good enough for God. That's what you've come to believe.

Well, I'm here to tell you that is a LIE! A ridiculous lie — one that has no truth to it at all. Like that $100 bill, your value isn't based on how you look at the moment. A $100 bill is still a $100 bill, even if it's got some dirt on it, or if it's a little wrinkly. Its value is still there.

The same is true for you. Your worth isn't dictated by how you look right now; you're like the $100 bill. Yeah, you may have seen better days in the past, but that doesn't mean that you're worthless. No matter what people say or think about you, your value never changes in God's eyes. You are His precious child and nothing will ever change that.

The daughter of the king is always the daughter of the king—regardless of whether she's wearing a fancy evening gown in royal blue, or a beat-up old sweat suit in navy blue. Her clothing isn't what determines her value; it's who she *IS* that determines her value.

Or more accurately, it's *WHOSE* she is that really matters.

NOW THAT'S A REAL CHANGE!

Changing our lives isn't about willpower or self-control. Changing our lives is about changing our self-image; it's about knowing who we are in God's eyes, and choosing to believe what He says about us, regardless of what anyone else says *(including what we may think about ourselves)*.

Knowing that God was near and intimately concerned about all the details of his life changed everything for Zacchaeus.

> Then Zacchaeus stood and said to the Lord, "Look, Lord, I give half of my goods to the poor; and if I have taken anything from anyone by false accusation, I restore fourfold." And Jesus said to him, "Today salvation has come to this house, because he also is a son of Abraham; for the Son of Man has come to seek and to save that which was lost." (Luke 19:8-10)

WOW! Now that's a change! Zacchaeus becomes a new man. The cheater becomes honest. The thief becomes generous. The selfish becomes selfless. And all that happened from that one brief encounter with Jesus—where Zacchaeus finally understood his value in God's eyes.

91

Fr. Anthony Messeh

A famous professional athlete was once asked how he was able to cope with all the pressure that comes with playing before large crowds, and the enormous expectations that surround him. He responded, *"I know that even if I completely blow it, my mom will still love me."*

I think God wants His children to learn the same lesson.

"The one who comes to Me I will by no means cast out."
(John 6:37)

PART THREE

GOD IS RELEVANT

*H*ave you ever seen a child open a gift?

When my daughter was three years old, she received an electronic keyboard—complete with a little pink stand and all kinds of bells and whistles. At first glance, I thought it seemed a bit advanced for my little preschooler, but what did I know?! Either way, it was too late now. Once she opened it and we put it together, she LOVED it and was ready to rock 'n' roll!

Now, what do you think she did next? How did she begin using her new toy? She'd never played with an electronic keyboard before, so how did she go about learning how it worked?

Did she read the instruction manual? Did she ask her five-year-old brother to see if he had any expertise? Did she go online and search for a YouTube video explaining how it works?

No! She did what any normal, red-blooded, three-year-old child would do . . . SHE STARTED PUSHING THE BUTTONS! As many buttons as she could, and all at once. Each time she pushed a button, something would happen: A noise would come out of the keyboard. That was cool! And then she'd push a *different* button and something *different* would happen . . . that was even cooler!

So, here's my daughter—three years old, never played a musical instrument in her life—but now she's jamming on the keyboard. She's rockin' 'n' rollin', and as far as she's concerned, Beethoven can move over because the next musical legend has now arrived!

I know we're only talking about a three-year-old here, but let's think about this logically.

Did she have any idea what she was doing? NO.

Did she use the keyboard properly, as it was designed to be used? NO, again.

Was she getting the *most* out of this new toy? Not even close! She wasn't even making music; it was just noise.

But to her, that really didn't matter. She was happy. She was pushing buttons and things were happening. She was seeing results. And as far as she was concerned, the results were pretty cool.

You know, we're kinda like that with God. Once we discover who God is and begin to form a relationship with Him, we're like a child with a new toy. We *THINK* we know what we're doing, and we *ASSUME* we have this "God-thing" figured out.

Yeah, this stuff is easy. Look, I prayed and something happened over here. Then I went to church and more stuff seems to be happening over there. And I'll bet if I go to church and pray at the same time, stuff will be happening everywhere! Yep, I pretty much got it figured out now.

We receive "the gift of God" and it knocks our socks off. We begin to understand His goodness, and we get a taste of His graciousness. We're blown away by the nearness of God and who we are in His eyes. Now, all of sudden, everything looks different. Life isn't the same. We now have something that we didn't have before: a real relationship with God.

And like my daughter—pushing all the buttons at the same time—we *think* we got this new toy figured out. We start pushing all the buttons we can: the "pray" button, the "Bible" button, the "help-old-ladies-cross-the-street" button. We push buttons and stuff happens, and as far as we're concerned, THIS IS GREAT!

But what happens when you push the "pray" button and nothing happens? What do you do then? Or what if you push the "Bible" button and nothing comes out—only silence? How will you deal with that? Or what happens when you go out of your way to push the "help-old-ladies-cross-the-street" button, and the result is that the old lady hits you on the head with her cane and steals your wallet? *(Never say never.)*

What then?

King Solomon, a man known for his wisdom and depth of understanding, once said:

> "For to know You is complete righteousness, and
> to know your power is the root of immortality."
> (Wisdom 15:3)

Having a relationship with God is the greatest gift you could ever hope to receive. The ability to "know God" and relate to Him as a Father is a prize that no man or woman can ever deserve. But that gift isn't always easy to figure out, is it? It doesn't always work the way we want it to. It can actually be quite confusing sometimes.

To get the most out of this gift, we need to dig a little deeper into how it works. In the first section of this book, we looked at how GOD IS REAL. He's a "HE," not an "IT." He's a good father, a gracious father, and a near father.

But now it's time for us to dive deeper into how that relationship is supposed to work. Many of us are operating out of *ASSUMPTION* in our relationship with God. We're like my daughter with her keyboard: we think we know what we're doing and how to use this gift. We're pushing buttons and seeing stuff happen.

But the truth is we are falling far short of what our relationship with God is supposed to be. There's potential for so much more! Knowing God is *"the root of immortality"* as King Solomon said. So it's time for us to stop *guessing*, and start *understanding* how He works.

And that gets us to section three of this book: GOD IS RELEVANT. Now that we know *who* God is, let's talk about how He operates.

CHAPTER 11

INVISIBLE YET INVINCIBLE

What happens when you plant a seed in the ground? Do you see it taking in nutrients from the soil? Do you see it extending its roots down into the earth? Do you see any action at all? Of course not! Eventually you'll see the final stages of its growth—the part that takes place above the soil—but the real action happens underneath, where our eyes cannot see.

Hold that thought—I'll come back to it in a minute.

Once upon a time, there was a wicked king named Nebuchadnezzar *(pronounced neh-bah-kuhd-NEZ-er)*. Nebuchadnezzar ruled over the Babylonian empire for more than 40 years in the 6th century BC. During his reign, he was the most feared and powerful man on earth. Nicknamed the "Destroyer of Nations," Nebuchadnezzar was a ruthless king who took delight in brutally destroying nations and mercilessly enslaving any of the survivors.

One of those nations that he conquered was Judah, the southern kingdom of Israel, where the people of God lived. Judah was home to Jerusalem, the holy city which housed the Temple of God. In other words, Jerusalem was the city God

Himself called home! That was enough to make other kings and rulers afraid to go to war against Judah.

Back in the ancient world, when nations went to war, it wouldn't just be a battle between armies; it was a battle between gods. So according to their belief, conquering Judah was equal to conquering the God of Judah Himself! And that's what Nebuchadnezzar did.

So, you can imagine that Nebuchadnezzar would be more than just a little proud of himself and his accomplishments. He had not only taken over the world, the "Destroyer of Nations" had even destroyed God's nation too!

He was the most powerful man in the most powerful empire in the world. And he wasn't bashful about letting everyone know it.

> At the end of the twelve months he was walking about the royal palace of Babylon. The king [Nebuchadnezzar] spoke, saying, "Is not this great Babylon, that I have built for a royal dwelling by my mighty power and for the honor of my majesty? (Daniel 4:29-30)

The world was his. He was sitting at the height of arrogance and pomp—and enjoying every minute of it. He had silenced his enemies and defeated all those who stood against him—including God Himself. He was living the good life . . .
. . . or so he thought.

> *While the word was still in the king's mouth,* a voice fell from heaven: "King Nebuchadnezzar, to you it is spoken: the kingdom has departed from you! And they shall drive you from men, and your dwelling shall be with the beasts of the field. They shall make

you eat grass like oxen; and seven times shall pass over you, *until you know that the Most High rules in the kingdom of men, and gives it to whomever He chooses."*

That very hour the word was fulfilled concerning Nebuchadnezzar; he was driven from men and ate grass like oxen; his body was wet with the dew of heaven till his hair had grown like eagles' feathers and his nails like birds' claws. (Daniel 4:31-33)

Excuse me . . . I beg your pardon . . . what just happened there? One minute Nebuchadnezzar is on top of the world—the destroyer of nations and ruler of the empire; even God Himself appeared defeated by the mighty king. The next minute he's completely lost his mind, humbled by the One he *thought* he had defeated! In the blink of an eye, God stepped in and everything changed.

Nebuchadnezzar was arrogant and foolish enough to think that he had defeated God and that he was now sovereign. He looked at his accomplishments and God's *seeming* lack of ability to stop him, and concluded that he was the invincible one, not God. But before he could get the sentence out of his mouth, God came out of nowhere, and Nebuchadnezzar learned a simple truth . . .

GOD IS ALWAYS IN CONTROL.

After losing his sanity and being driven out of the city by his own people, Nebuchadnezzar lived in the wild like an animal for seven years. The proud king had been humbled, while the One who had been silent (God) finally spoke.

After the seven years were complete, God restored Nebuchadnezzar's sanity, and Nebuchadnezzar had a new appreciation for the God whom He couldn't see.

> And at the end of the time I, Nebuchadnezzar, lifted
> my eyes to heaven, and my understanding returned
> to me; and I blessed the Most High and praised and
> honored Him who lives forever:
> For His dominion is an everlasting dominion,
> and His kingdom is from generation to genera-
> tion. All the inhabitants of the earth are reputed as
> nothing; He does according to His will in the army
> of heaven and among the inhabitants of the earth.
> No one can restrain His hand or say to Him, "What
> have You done?" (Daniel 4:34-35)

Nebuchadnezzar learned his lesson. He discovered that even though you may not always be able to see it or feel it, God is in full control — every minute of every day. Not a moment goes by where God doesn't hold the entire universe and all its inhabitants in the palm of His hand.

You may think your life is out of control — and it may very well be out of *YOUR* control — but nothing is ever outside of *GOD'S CONTROL*.

Just ask Nebuchadnezzar.

GOD'S SILENCE ≠ GOD'S ABSENCE

> [God] is He who sits above the circle of the earth,
> and its inhabltants are like grasshoppers, who
> stretches out the heavens like a curtain, and spreads
> them out like a tent to dwell in. He brings the princes
> to nothing; He makes the judges of the earth useless.
> (Isaiah 40:22-23)

There's a control freak inside all of us, isn't there? We like to be in control. We like knowing that our lives are headed in the right direction, according to some type of plan — preferably the plan we came up with. Nothing's better than sitting down with a notepad, coming up with a 5-year plan, and then marching our way through that plan, one day at a time . . . checking off lots of little boxes along the way!

But that isn't life. Life rarely goes according to plan—at least not according to *OUR* plan. It's usually one unexpected and unplanned event after the next—one *"this-wasn't-sup-posed-to-happen-God"* moment after another:

- Your boss embarrasses you in an email and ruins your reputation.
- Your "friend" spreads a rumor behind your back.
- Your parents—the ones you look to for protection—abuse you and hurt you.
- Your wife gets diagnosed with cancer.

It's easy to look at life and throw your hands up in the air and feel like it's completely out of control. But is it? Is the world *really* out of control? Or is it just out of *YOUR* control?

When Nebuchadnezzar was king, it certainly seemed like life was out of control. I'm sure the people of Judah thought God was just watching while they fell into the hands of the wicked king. But God was there the whole time. He never lost control for one second! He was there and just waiting for the right moment to act.

That teaches us a valuable lesson when it comes to living in a relationship with God: GOD'S SILENCE ≠ GOD'S ABSENCE.

Just because you can't hear God speaking doesn't mean He isn't speaking. Just because you can't see God working doesn't mean He isn't working. And just because you can't see anything happening doesn't mean that nothing's happening. IT JUST MEANS YOU CAN'T SEE IT!

Remember the analogy of the seed at the start of this chapter? Not seeing the seed grow doesn't mean it isn't growing. Not seeing anything happen doesn't mean nothing is happening. It simply means you can't see it.

The same holds true when it comes to God's work in our lives and in the world today. God's silence does not equal God's absence.

I know it might not always seem like it, but God is always working in your life—even right now, at this very minute. He's actively at work, making things happen, in full control. And I don't mean that in the sense that He's just keeping all the planets from colliding or making sure the Sun doesn't get too close and burn us all up (although those seem like pretty important functions as well). I mean, God is working in the day-by-day, hour-by-hour, minute-by-minute details of your life in such a way to bring you closer to Him and closer to His "good" plan for your life.

He knows where you are and He knows where you need to be, and right now, at this very minute, He is working to help you get one step closer.

THE GREAT MAESTRO OF THE UNIVERSE

Think of God like the conductor of a symphony—aka, the maestro. I used to always wonder why those guys got so much credit; it doesn't seem like their job is too difficult. I mean, they aren't the ones making any of the music. They don't even stand on stage. They're usually just below the stage with their backs to the audience, just waving their arms back and forth. How hard could that be?

But I later realized that the maestro is actually the one controlling the entire show. He raises his arms, and the music begins. He swings his hands back and forth, and sets the tempo. He raises one hand, and the strings know to increase their volume; he lowers that same hand, and they return to silence. He motions with the other hand, and the bass kicks in. His eyes shift toward the trumpets in the back, and with just the raise of an eyebrow, they know to get ready as well.

There may be times where certain sections of the orchestra feel forgotten or ignored. They may think to themselves, *"Why doesn't he look my way?"* or *"When is it my turn?"* But if they're willing to wait patiently, they'll soon realize that the maestro is just waiting for the exact right moment before inviting them to join in.

At all times, all eyes are on him, and he keeps everything working together in harmony.

That's God!

He's there the whole time; He never takes a break. Even when you can't see Him or feel Him, He's there. He's always there and He's always in control. The symphony conductor controls the entire orchestra without ever playing a single musical note or even picking up an instrument. In fact, you often don't even realize he's there till the end when he walks onto the stage.

But that doesn't mean that he isn't in full control.

Same with God. His silence does not mean His absence. Regardless of what you see (or don't see), God is working. Like the conductor, His best work won't be what you see up on stage, but rather the hidden work done behind the scenes. That's where He makes great things happen.

Don't believe me? Take a listen to this next story and see for yourself.

SUSANNA'S STORY

If you've never heard the story of Susanna, you're missing out. It might just be the most uplifting and inspirational story in the entire Bible.[1] It's got all you could ask for in a story: courtroom drama, scandalous lies, Peeping Toms, and of course, attempted blackmail. But more than that, it's a story of hope — hope that God is in full control no matter what the circumstances might be.

The main character is a beautiful Hebrew woman named Susanna, a righteous, God-fearing woman who is wife to a man named Joakim. One day, Susanna goes into her garden to bathe, as was her custom to do. Before disrobing, she asks her maids to lock the gate on their way out so that she can bathe in privacy. But once the gate is closed, she soon realizes that she's not alone.

Two perverted and lustful old men — elders of good reputation who were appointed to serve as judges over God's people — had been secretly desiring Susanna for some time now. After Susanna's maids left, they decide to sneak into the garden to catch a glimpse of Susanna up close and personal.

---

[1] The reason you've probably never heard of Susanna is because her story isn't contained in most Bibles circulated today. It appears in a subset of books commonly referred to as the Deuterocanonical books—a set of books/passages that are considered canonical by the Orthodox Church, as well as the Catholic Church. These books, which have been widely accepted since the earliest days of Christianity, include three more chapters to the book of Daniel; it's in those three chapters that we find Susanna's beautiful story.

> As soon as the maids had left, the two old men got up
> and ran to her. "Look," they said, "the garden doors
> are shut, no one can see us, and we want you. So
> give in to our desire, and lie with us. If you refuse,
> we will testify against you that a young man was
> here with you and that is why you sent your maids
> away." (Daniel 13:19-21)

Talk about dirty old men . . . these guys tell Susanna that either she sleeps with them or they will tell everyone that they found her committing adultery with a young man in the garden. So her choices are either to commit adultery with the two men— or to be accused of committing adultery with someone else!

What should she do? What *CAN* she do? Should she stick to her morals and resist the two men? But doing so means death since the punishment for a woman convicted of adultery was to be stoned. She could maybe try to convince the courts that she's innocent, but they'd surely believe the testimony of the elders over hers. The two men were JUDGES, for goodness sake!

Her only options are to either give in and commit sin with the two men, or resist them and face death by stoning.

> "I am completely trapped," Susanna groaned. "If I
> yield, it will be my death; if I refuse, I cannot escape
> your power. Yet it is better for me not to do it and
> to fall into your power than to sin before the Lord."
> (Daniel 13:22-23)

Susanna sticks to her morals; she refuses to be blackmailed into committing sin. She trusts in God. She decides that she'd rather have God on her side vs. these two dirty old men. She tells them NO!

Now surely God will save her, right? For sure He'll do something, right? If I was in Susanna's shoes, I'd be thinking: *"God, I made the right choice and trusted in You; so therefore, I am sure You will do something mighty and amazing and supernatural! There's no way that You will allow them to accuse me and ruin my reputation. There's no way You'll allow the other judges to believe them; the judges will see straight through their lies at once. I just know it!"*

The next day comes. The two old men gather an assembly together and call for Susanna to be brought out. They publicly accuse her of committing adultery as they said they would.

> In the midst of the people the two old men rose up and laid their hands on her head. As she wept she looked up to heaven, for she trusted in the Lord wholeheartedly. (Daniel 13:34-35)

"She trusted in the Lord wholeheartedly." WOW! I love that verse!

> The old men said, "As we were walking in the garden alone, this woman entered with two servant girls, shut the garden gates and sent the servant girls away. A young man, who was hidden there, came and lay with her. When we, in a corner of the garden, saw this lawlessness, we ran toward them. We saw them lying together, but the man we could not hold, because he was stronger than we; he opened the gates and ran off. Then we seized this one and asked who the young man was, but she refused to tell us. We testify to this." (Daniel 13:36-41a)

Oh man, if two old guys ever deserved a punch in the face, it's these guys! They lied straight through their teeth and said that Susanna committed adultery. But God's in control, right? There's no way that He'll allow the assembly to believe these guys . . . there's no way He'll allow Susanna to be condemned unjustly . . . right?

> The assembly believed them, since they were elders and judges of the people, and they condemned her to death. (Daniel 13:41b)

Uh-oh. That isn't how it was supposed to go.

The plan was supposed to be that Susanna trusted in God, and then God rescued Susanna. That's how it was supposed to happen. Why would God allow the assembly to believe them? Why didn't He do something? Did He fall asleep on the job? I thought He was supposed to be in full control? Where is He now when Susanna is getting sentenced to death?

WAKE UP GOD!!!

Remember the key principle from earlier? God's silence ≠ God's absence.

Susanna, do you hear/see/feel God doing anything? *"Nothing."*

Susanna, does that mean that He *actually* isn't doing anything? *"Nope. I know that God's silence does not mean God's absence. He may be silent, but I know He's working!"*

God's ways are not always apparent, but as Susanna soon finds out, they sure are EFFECTIVE!

TRUSTING IN GOD'S HANDS

> But Susanna cried aloud: "Eternal God, you know what is hidden and are aware of all things before they come to be: you know that they have testified falsely against me. Here I am about to die, though

I have done none of the things for which these men
have condemned me." (Daniel 13:42-43)

That's incredible! Susanna still trusts in God. She doesn't
complain or grumble or get bitter. She knows that He holds the
world in the palm of His hand, and no person or circumstance is
ever outside of that. She knows that her life is not in the hands
of those dirty old men, or in the hands of that court; her life is
not in the hands of the circumstances that happened upon her.

Her life is in the hands of the Almighty God—the Maestro
of the universe, who controls all things and *"makes all things
work together for good to those who love God."* She trusts
that even though God has been silent thus far, He certainly
isn't absent! He is still on His throne and He controls the universe—including those old men and the court in front of which
she stands.

She believes in God's invisible, yet invincible Hand. She
trusts that He won't leave her. And boy was she right!

> The Lord heard her prayer. *As she was being led to
> execution,* God stirred up the holy spirit of a young
> boy named Daniel, and he cried aloud: "I am inno-
> cent of this woman's blood." (Daniel 13:44-46)

"As she was being led to execution," a young man named
Daniel interrupts the proceedings. At the time, Daniel isn't the
great prophet that he eventually will become; right now, he's
just a young boy that God brings onto the scene, seemingly out
of nowhere. God has given Daniel a spirit of wisdom, and now
He calls him into action at just the right time.

Can you see how the Maestro is working?

All the people turned and asked him, "What are you saying?" He stood in their midst and said, "Are you such fools, you Israelites, to condemn a daughter of Israel without investigation and without clear evidence? Return to court, for they have testified falsely against her." (Daniel 13:47-49)

Daniel then asks the assembly to separate the two old men so that he can examine them properly, and he asks them about the details of what they had witnessed:

"Now, then, if you were a witness, tell me under what tree you saw them together."
"Under a mastic tree," he answered. "Your fine lie has cost you your head," said Daniel; "for the angel of God has already received the sentence from God and shall split you in two."
Putting him to one side, he ordered the other one to be brought . . . "Now, then, tell me under what tree you surprised them together."
"Under an oak," he said. "Your fine lie has cost you also your head," said Daniel; "for the angel of God waits with a sword to cut you in two so as to destroy you both."
The whole assembly cried aloud, blessing God who saves those who hope in him. (Daniel 13:54-60)

WOW! Now that's how you do it! Bravo! The Maestro needs to take a bow because that was incredible!!!

Susanna was on her way to execution; the old men had convinced everyone that she was guilty. But little did they know that the Great Maestro was working behind the scenes, stirring up the spirit of a young lad named Daniel. Then Daniel came out of nowhere and saved the day; Susanna was delivered, and those dirty old men were condemned to the same death sentence they attempted to place on Susanna.

UNBELIEVABLE!

What's the moral of the story? Simple. Your life—like Susanna's life—is not in the hands of men, nor is it in the hands of circumstances. It might seem that way at times—especially when God is silent, but we know that His silence does not mean His absence. Your life is in the hands of Almighty God and no one else.

Repeat this phrase whenever you're feeling that your life is out of control: *"At all times and in all circumstances, my life is fully in the hands of God."*

Your life is not in your boss's hands—even though it may seem like it at times. Your life is fully in the hands of God.

Your life is not in the hands of the stock market—even though you're depending on it for your future. Your life is fully in the hands of God.

Your life is not in the hands of the circumstances of your life—no matter how painful and hurtful they may be. YOUR LIFE IS FULLY IN THE HANDS OF GOD!

"At all times and in all circumstances, my life is fully in the hands of God."

As the Great Maestro of the universe, God is always working. He's orchestrating events and circumstances in ways that we'll never understand. Now that doesn't mean that we're just robots and we have no control over our lives—absolutely not! We'll deal with that point in the next chapter.

But what it does mean is that your life isn't a random series of events or circumstances; it's a story being written by God. God never left Susanna at any time; He was writing her life story, even when she didn't realize it. And He's doing the same in your life too.

Why? Because He's not just the Maestro of the universe, He's also the Maestro of your life.

"Who is he who speaks and it comes to pass, when the Lord has not commanded it? Is it not from the mouth of the Most High that woe and well-being proceed?"
Lamentations 3:37-38

CHAPTER 12

LEARNING TO BLAME GOD

*I*n the last chapter, we learned that at all times and in all circumstances, our lives are fully in the hands of God. That should inevitably lead you to ask:

If my life is fully in God's hands and He is in complete control at all times, then does it make a difference what I do? Does it matter if I choose A or B if the whole thing is in God's hands anyway? If He has FULL control, then that means that I have ZERO control, right?

Logically that seems to make sense. You can't have two people driving one car. The more control one person has, the less control the other one has. If one has *full* control, then the other must have *zero* control. So therefore, it would appear—based on the last chapter—that God is the one in the driver's seat, and we're all just helplessly along for the ride.

Not exactly.

Yes, God is in full control over my life; He is the great conductor of the universe. But the conductor's control doesn't negate the musician's ability (or need) to cooperate. The conductor can wave his hands all he wants, but in the end, it's up to the guys playing the instruments to cooperate and make the music.

The same holds true with God.

Yes, God is in full control. He is sovereign, meaning He reigns supreme over all. But His sovereignty doesn't mean that we have no role; in fact, for His sovereignty to function as it was meant, it must be complemented by our *cooperation*.

Think of a king ruling a country. The king is sovereign in his land. He has the ability to do as he pleases and he's in full control. But his control doesn't eliminate the people's ability to choose whether to cooperate with his sovereignty or not. They can choose to obey his laws or disobey them. They can choose to pay their taxes or withhold them. They can accept his authority and bow humbly in front of him as he passes by — or they can choose to resist his authority and suffer the consequences.

Every individual in the kingdom must choose: Cooperate with the king's sovereignty and reap the benefits (e.g., military protection, freedom, etc.), or resist his sovereignty and reap the consequences *(big trouble!)*. Everyone must choose.

In much the same manner, we have a choice when it comes to God's sovereignty. If we want to reap the benefits, we must *CHOOSE* to cooperate.

> Trust in the Lord with all your heart, and lean not on your own understanding; in all your ways acknowledge Him, and He shall direct your paths. (Proverbs 3:5-6)

Like the conductor and the king in my earlier examples, God's control never negates our ability to respond. He is in full control and is ready to guide us according to His good plan, but it's up to us to choose to listen and act accordingly. We must *"acknowledge Him"* if we want Him to *"direct our paths."*

THE GIFT (AND RESPONSIBILITY) OF FREE WILL

As a gracious Father, when God created man back in the Garden of Eden, He gave him many gifts:
He gave man authority over all the animals.

> Have dominion over the fish of the sea, over the birds of the air, and over every living thing that moves on the earth. (Genesis 1:28)

He gave man a perfect home to live in.

> The Lord God planted a garden eastward in Eden, and there He put the man whom He had formed. And out of the ground the Lord God made every tree grow that is pleasant to the sight and good for food. (Genesis 2:8-9)

He gave man the most beautiful gift of all when He created "WO-man."

> "This is now bone of my bones and flesh of my flesh; she shall be called Woman, because she was taken out of Man" . . . And they were both naked, the man and his wife, and were not ashamed. (Genesis 2:23, 25)

But there's another valuable gift that we often overlook:

> "Let Us make man in Our image, according to Our likeness." (Genesis 1:26)

Being made in the image of God means that we've been given the gift of FREE WILL—the ability to make choices and the responsibility of dealing with the consequences of those choices. God didn't *have to* give us free will; He could have done it differently. He could have made it so that we *must obey* Him, but He didn't.

That's because God doesn't want robots to just follow His instructions. He doesn't want pets to sit at His feet and obey Him all day long. He wants children. He wants sons and daughters. He wants love. So instead of making Adam His slave, God chose instead to make him His son. That's where the gift of free will comes from.

But free will isn't just about the freedom to choose, it's also about the responsibility to face consequences. Remember Romans 8:28?

> And we know that all things work together for good
> to those who love God. (Romans 8:28)

We talked earlier about how God is always working to make *"all things work together for good."* Even the bad situations of life—the ones that appear to have no good in them—He finds a way to make them *work together* for good. He can do that because He is the Sovereign Ruler of all—the Great Maestro of the universe and of your life.

But there's a caveat: The promise doesn't apply to everyone and to every situation. It has a condition that must first be fulfilled.

The promise is *"All things work together for good"*— that's what we want; the condition is *"to those who love God"*—that's what HE wants. You can't have the promise without the condition. In other words, we can't say that everything in this world is always working together for good in everyone's life. We want to say that because it makes us feel warm and fuzzy inside, but that's not what the verse says. The verse clearly stipulates the condition to the promise: *"to those who love God."*

What does that mean? I love God, don't I? How can I tell? Doesn't everyone love God? And even if they don't love God, doesn't God love everyone? So why wouldn't He just make this promise apply to everyone? Why be selective?

Back to the example about cooperating with a ruler's sovereignty. The king *wants* to protect his people. He *wants* them all to be loyal subjects. He *wants* them all to abide by the laws of his country. But it isn't his choice! They have the free will to choose whether to cooperate or not. If they choose to resist, then they relinquish all the benefits that come with being a member of that country.

Or think back to the example of the conductor. The conductor promises to signal the musicians when they should begin. He promises to control the volume and make sure that all the instruments can be heard. He promises that the final production will sound beautiful in the end. But those promises are all based on a condition: YOU MUST LOOK AT THE CONDUCTOR AND OBEY HIS INSTRUCTIONS!

If you fail to fulfill the condition, you shouldn't be surprised if you don't realize the promise.

One more time: *"And we know that all things work together for good to those who love God."*

This is where our choice comes in. In the last chapter, we saw how God worked behind the scenes to save Susanna at the last minute. We also saw how God humbled the evil King Nebuchadnezzar when it seemed like he was on top of the world. We know that God is always working in our lives to bring us closer to where He knows we need to be.

We know all that.

But knowing all about God's sovereignty does you no good unless you choose to *COOPERATE* with it.

If you cooperate *a little*, then *a little* of the things in your life are working together for good.

If you cooperate *a lot*, then *a lot* of the things in your life are working together for good.

And if you don't cooperate at all—resisting God and resisting His authority in your life—then *NONE* of the things in your life are working together for good.

Sorry. That's not an opinion; it's the truth.

THIS IS ALL YOUR FAULT, GOD!

Let me warn you: What I'm about to say *sounds* bad. At best, it comes across as irreverent and disrespectful; at worst, it borders on the brink of blasphemous. But I believe it's the key to understanding what it means to *"cooperate"* with God's sovereignty, so I'm going to say it anyway!

(If you thought I was at risk of getting hit by lightning before, wait till you get a load of this!)

If the only way we're going to realize the promise of *"all things work together for good"* is by cooperating with God's sovereignty, then we need a practical application of how to do that. All too often, we speak in philosophical terms about "loving God," and "surrendering to God," and "giving my life to Jesus", without having any idea what that means and how that makes a difference in our lives.

What does it mean to cooperate with God's sovereignty? What is that supposed to look like on a day-to-day basis? How do I know if I'm doing it or not?

There are many ways you could answer that question, but I want to focus on just one. Here goes . . . cue the lightning . . .

Learn to BLAME GOD.

Yep, that's right. Learn to blame God. It sounds bad to say that (and it looks even worse when you read it), but it's the truth. The key to cooperating with God's sovereignty, and thereby laying hold of *"all things working together for good"* in your life, is learning to blame God for the things that are happening.

Huh?

First of all, let's define the word "blame." Maybe I define it a bit differently than you do. Most people use "blame" in a negative context, assigning fault for a certain wrongdoing:

- *"I blame you for ruining our marriage."*
- *"All the problems in the country today can be blamed on the President."*
- *"I blame God for this illness and the condition that I'm in."*

We use "blame" to mean "accuse someone of wrongdoing." That's NOT the kind of "blaming God" that I'm talking about—not at all!

The real meaning of "blame" is actually "to hold responsible." So we blame God when we hold Him responsible for the things that are happening in our lives. Not that God's responsible for *causing all* those things—remember we have free will, and those who hurt us have free will too—but rather that He's responsible for *solving* them and finding a way to make them work for good in our lives.

By *that* definition, I absolutely think we should learn to blame God more often:

> *"God, I believe that You are ultimately responsible for where I am in life, and I know You'll get me through it. I could focus on what my parents did, or what my boss did, or what I didn't do to bring this pain into my life, but instead I choose to focus on what You WILL DO to heal it. I am choosing to look to You and blame YOU and nobody else."*

That might be the healthiest thing you could ever do. Why?

If I think my parents are responsible for my situation, then I'll look to them to fix it. If I think my wife is responsible for my situation, then I'll look to her to fix it. If I think the economy is responsible for my situation, then I'll look to nobody to fix it, and probably end up feeling frustrated and hopeless.

But if I hold God responsible for my problem—not responsible for the cause, but responsible for the solution—then I end up looking to Him for healing as well. BINGO!

God may not be the cause of all the bad things in my life, but He is willing to be the solution. Wanna see how that works? Meet Joseph.

JOSEPH: THE FRUIT OF BLAMING GOD

What's the worst thing you've ever done to a sibling? The angriest you've ever been with a brother or sister or even a cousin?

Growing up in a house with two brothers, we had our fair share of "fights" *(usually centered around video games and ping-pong matches)*. But they were sibling fights, not real fights. In real fights, you try to hurt each other. But when you fight your sibling, there's something in the back of your mind that tells you, *"He's your brother; you're not really trying to hurt him, just trying to send a message."*

There are limits to what is supposed to happen in sibling fights.

Well, apparently that wasn't the case for a guy named Joseph and his family back in the Old Testament. Joseph was the second youngest of 12 brothers. He was always favored by his father, but hated by his brothers. One day, Joseph went out to meet his ten older brothers as they were working in the field.

> Now when they saw him afar off, even before he came near them, they conspired against him to kill him. (Genesis 37:18)

That's not a very good start to the story—conspiracy to murder right off the bat. I'm pretty sure that breaks Sibling Fight Rule #1.

> So it came to pass, when Joseph had come to his brothers, that they stripped Joseph of his tunic, the tunic of many colors that was on him. Then they took him and cast him into a pit. And the pit was empty; there was no water in it. (Genesis 37:23-24)

And there goes Rule #2!

Fighting? Okay. Throwing your brother into a pit? Not okay. Planning to trick your younger brother? Okay. Conspiring to murder him? Not okay . . . very, very, very not okay.

And you know what's even worse? What did the brothers do *after* they threw their younger brother into the pit and left him there for dead?

You'd think that maybe they'd feel a little remorse . . . or a little guilt. I'm sure Joseph was screaming and pleading with them to save him: *"Guys! I'm your brother! Don't do this to me! Please!!!"* That would probably be enough to make most people sick to their stomach.

Not Joseph's brothers.

> And they sat down to eat a meal. (Genesis 37:25)

Can you imagine that? Getting thrown into a pit is bad enough. Getting thrown in by your brothers is even worse. Getting thrown in by your brothers who then proceed to have lunch while you're screaming for your life is awful! Downright AWFUL!

What would you do if you were Joseph at the bottom of that pit? What would you say? If there's anyone who's ever had the right to blame God in the wrong way—saying, *"This is your fault, God!"*—it's Joseph. He could have blamed God for giving him evil brothers. He could have blamed Him for making his father so clueless about what was going on with his family. He could have gotten angry that God did nothing to stop his brothers' plan.

But he didn't. He never blamed God in a bad way—only in a healthy way.

Somewhere along the way, Joseph learned to look UP instead of looking OUT. He held God ultimately responsible for this circumstance, not his brothers. He looked to God for the solution, not His brothers. At some point, early in his life,

Joseph made the decision to view God as the Maestro of the universe and of his life, and to hold Him 100% responsible for whatever circumstances came his way.

And that decision made all the difference. It allowed him to reap the benefits of God's sovereignty.

Fast forward to the end of Joseph's life. By this time, God has delivered Joseph from the pit, sent him to Egypt as a slave, and turned "Joseph, the slave," into "Joseph, the second most powerful man in all of Egypt." All in a day's work for the Great Maestro!

Eventually, Joseph ends up meeting his brothers face-to-face. They come to Egypt in need of help because their land was in famine. They meet Joseph and are understandably terrified of what he will do to them.

Now is Joseph's chance to get revenge. Now he's strong and they are weak. Most people would be thinking to themselves: *"These guys hurt me, and I blame them for all the problems that I endured in my life. Now it's time to get even."*

But not Joseph. Listen to the man who made a habit of "blaming God" in the right way:

> "But as for you, you meant evil against me; but God meant it for good, in order to bring it about as it is this day, to save many people alive." (Genesis 50:20)

WOW! Amazing! Truly, truly amazing! I know people who haven't experienced 1% of the hurt that Joseph endured and would never be able to say those words.

Why? Because they haven't yet learned to blame God.

THE BEST THING THAT EVER HAPPENED TO ME

It wasn't by chance that Joseph fell into that pit; it wasn't just because his brothers were cruel and cold-blooded. We agreed that our lives are not in the hands of men or of circumstances, but rather at ALL times and in ALL circumstances, our lives are FULLY in the hands of God. The words "ALL" and "FULLY" don't leave much wiggle room.

If we believe that, then we have to believe that God knew Joseph would be thrown into a pit, and He allowed it. And, most importantly, He would ultimately use that event for good in Joseph's life.

That last part is the tough one; don't skim over it too quickly. We have to believe that God will ultimately use every event for good in our lives.

Do you believe that the hardships and trials—even though they may not always be *CAUSED* by God—can always be *USED* by God for good in your life?

Forgive me for what I'm about to say—I know it sounds rude and insensitive—but I wouldn't say it unless I really believed that it has the power to bring healing and freedom to many who are overburdened with anger, bitterness, and resentment.

Is it possible that the very thing you complain about most— the thing you wish never happened—is it possible that this circumstance could be used by God for good in your life?

I know it sounds bad; it sounds like I'm making light of your problems. It sounds like I'm saying, *"Suck it up, Buttercup, and move on with life."*

BUT I'M NOT! I'm not saying that at all. I'm actually saying the exact opposite. I'm saying that you CANNOT move on with your life until you find healing for your pain, or resolution for your guilt, or freedom from your burdens. I don't want you to *ignore* your situation and look the other way; I want you to *address* it and look at it in a *God-blaming* sort of way.

Is that possible? Is it possible for the teenager who was molested by a relative? Is it possible for the single mother who had to bury her child because of a drunk driver? Is it possible for the children who walked into their house one day and saw both of their parents dead, lying in a pool of blood, the result of one parent killing the other and then committing suicide—is it possible for them?

Is it really possible to look at those situations and say, *"I trust God will bring good out of it"?*

Yes, I say yes. God says yes. And Joseph says yes too. The answer is YES!

Why? Because *"we know all things work together for good to those who love God."* Don't treat that as just a nice saying or an inspirational quote. It's a promise from God's mouth. And if He promised it, then He will deliver it! He is the Great Maestro, and He can take any situation—no matter how bad it may seem—and use it to bring forth good.

We need to stop thinking: *"If only _____ didn't happen to me, then my life would be completely different."* Stop blaming people or circumstances or even yourself. God is the Great Maestro who is actively working at all times. Your life is never in the hands of men or in the hands of circumstances, but rather, at ALL times and in ALL circumstances, your life is FULLY in the hands of God.

Are you willing to believe that? Are you willing to trust God and blame Him for whatever circumstance you're going through?

I know this isn't an easy concept to believe; it goes against our very nature and how we've been living for many years. So maybe now is a good time to put this book down, close your eyes, and say a short prayer. Agreeing with me that God will make good out of your circumstances isn't the same as closing your eyes and telling God that you believe it.

"Lord, I trust You. I believe that You make all things work together for good to those who love You. I love You God and I trust that You'll make _____ work out for good in my life too. Please help me to trust You more and more every single day."

CHAPTER 13

WHEN GOD MESSES UP
YOUR PLANS

"A man's heart plans his way, but the Lord directs his steps."
(Proverbs 16:9)

*H*ave you ever wondered why it's so hard to trust God? It seems like it should be a lot easier than it is. After all, He's GOD! He knows what He's doing, doesn't He? Why is it such a struggle for us to trust Him and trust His plan?

I spoke earlier about how much of a control freak I am, and how much I like having things planned out and on paper. My motto is *"If it isn't written down, then it probably won't happen."* So for me, the hardest part of trusting God and His plan isn't the *"trusting"* part, it's the *"His plan"* part. I trust God 100%—that's not the issue. It's His plan that I'm not so sure about.

Let me explain.

I like plans. No, you don't understand . . . I *really* like plans. I like making plans and following plans. I like having goals and subgoals, deadlines, and project plans—these are the things that make my heart happy. I take great joy in setting challenging goals and then coming up with a plan to chip away at them a little bit every day. And then I especially like looking back at the end of the process and saying, *"YES! I did it!"*

What can I say . . . I love plans!

So again, when it comes to trusting God and trusting His plan, the part that I really struggle with isn't the "trusting God" part, it's the "trusting His plan" part. Why?

Because . . . I'm sorry to say this, but it's true . . . GOD KEEPS MESSING UP THE PLAN!

Or I guess what I should say is, God keeps messing up *MY* plan.

Here's what I find myself thinking at times: *"Why did God do that? That wasn't supposed to happen. That wasn't part of the plan. Did God change the plan? If so, how come He didn't send out a copy of the new plan in advance so that I can be prepared? Isn't it good to be prepared? Why keep me guessing all the time, wondering what's next? Doesn't God know that He's messing up the plan?"*

Apparently, God isn't as obsessed with my plan as I am.

THAT WASN'T PART OF THE PLAN, GOD!

Meet Jack, an older gentleman who's spent most of his life in the rural parts of Western Pennsylvania. Everyone who knows Jack absolutely loves him. He's honest, straightforward, and as reliable as can be. He has a strong personal relationship with God as well, and has always lived a virtuous and charitable life.

After 37 years of working hard in the lumber yards, Jack is entering a new phase in his life: he is getting ready to retire. There are some aspects of retired life that he absolutely can't wait for, specifically the slower pace and the relaxed lifestyle. Jack has longed to slow down and live a quieter life for years now, and he is finally about to get his chance. On the other hand, there are some aspects that he isn't so excited about.

Jack lives alone; he's been living alone ever since his wife passed away several years ago. He has three grown boys, but they moved out a long time ago. Jack is on his own now, and he needs to come up with a plan for the next phase of his life.

It's always been in Jack's mind to serve God till the day he dies. He isn't content to just retire and play card games all day; he wants to help others, and be a blessing to others as long as God gives him the ability to do so. But he knows that he can't do it alone. He needs help; he needs a partner.

That's why he's been contemplating the idea of getting remarried—not for the romantic involvement, but more for the companionship. He wants to find someone he can grow old with, and with whom he can serve God.

So he's been praying. And then he prays some more. And he keeps on praying. He doesn't want to make this decision on his own; he wants it to be God's decision. Jack is perfectly satisfied living on his own, but he feels that he needs someone to support him if he is going to serve God in the long term. And while praying, he has felt God encouraging the idea as well—which makes sense. After all, Jack isn't getting remarried for selfish purposes; he's doing it so he's better able to serve God.

Jack feels good about the idea, and God has given him peace about it. And he's had even more peace after meeting Emma, a beautiful woman who also wants to dedicate her life to serving God. And oddly enough, Emma isn't too interested in the romantic stuff either, so it's a perfect match! They both just want to serve God and dedicate their lives to Him.

So now, the plan is complete. Jack knows how he is going to spend the rest of his days. He will marry Emma, and they will live a quiet, peaceful life. She'll take care of him and be his support, and he'll do the same for her. And they both will serve God till the very end.

Ah! The perfect plan! Go ahead and put it in writing, Jack! Uhhh. . . on second thought . . . you might want to hold off on the writing for just a minute.

It's now one week before the wedding, and Jack has found out that Emma is pregnant (and Jack is not the father—that's for SURE!). God has told Jack not to worry, and to still marry Emma and help her raise the child.

"But that wasn't part of the plan, God."

Now three weeks before the baby is due, God tells Jack that he needs to leave Western Pennsylvania (the place he's lived his whole life) and move across the country to Los Angeles. He needs to pack up his 8-months pregnant wife and all their belongings, and drive their little hybrid hatchback across the country.

"But that REALLY wasn't part of the plan, God."

After living in Los Angeles for two years—and just starting to get settled—God tells Jack that it's time for him to move once again. It's time to go back to Pennsylvania. But this time, knowing that the hatchback is on its last leg and can't handle another cross-country trip, Jack and his family are instructed to take the bus instead of driving.

"That's it! My plan is officially ruined! God ruined it once again!"

How would you feel if you were in Jack's shoes? Doesn't he have the right to be a little upset? He had the perfect plan and God completely ruined it. Why would God do that to him?

Jack's story is one that we all know. You've probably figured out by now that it isn't a true story; the names, places, and details are all contrived—but the lesson is not. We all know what it's like to have a plan today, and then have God change it tomorrow. God seems to be guiding you in a certain direction, and then before you know it . . . BOOM! The rug gets pulled out from under you. Everything changes and you need a new plan quick.

As a friend of mine once told me: *"God shifts gears before I've even had a chance to sit down in the passenger seat."*

Why does He do that?

THE STORY OF JOSEPH
. . . NO, THE *OTHER* JOSEPH

Jack's story wasn't true, but it sounds an awful lot like one that is. The story I'm referring to is that of Joseph from the Bible—but not the same Joseph from the Bible that we met earlier. This is a completely different Joseph *(it was a popular name, I guess.)*

That Joseph (the first one) lived in the Old Testament, but *this* Joseph (the second one) lived in the New Testament. *That* Joseph first appears in the Bible as a young child, but *this* Joseph walks onto the Biblical stage as an old man—probably 80 or even 90 years old when we first meet him!

That Joseph wore a famous multicolor coat and is easily identifiable by most Bible readers, but *this* Joseph receives very little attention or fanfare, and isn't usually more than an *"extra"* in the annual Christmas pageant.

We don't know too much about *this* Joseph. But we know enough to learn how we should respond when God messes up our plans.

Like Jack in the fictitious story, Joseph is an old man, in the twilight of his life. It was the custom at the time that an old widower, like Joseph, would go to the Temple and find a virgin to take as his bride, a young girl who had taken a vow of virginity and offered herself to the service of the Lord. The purpose of the marriage was never sexual or romantic in any way—so get rid of the Hollywood idea of Joseph and Mary being like Romeo and Juliet. The guy was close to 90 years old for goodness' sake!

Joseph finds a bride named Mary and gets engaged. His plan is to slow down and live a peaceful life. He doesn't need money, he doesn't need romance, and he especially doesn't need HEADACHE! He just wants to slow down, take it easy, and quietly ride off into the sunset.

So, what's the first thing that happens to Joseph after he makes his plan?

> . . . Mary was betrothed to Joseph, before they came together, she was found with child of the Holy Spirit. Then Joseph her husband, being a just man, and not wanting to make her a public example, was minded to put her away secretly. But while he thought about these things, behold, an angel of the Lord appeared to him in a dream, saying, "Joseph, son of David, do not be afraid to take to you Mary your wife, for that which is conceived in her is of the Holy Spirit." (Matthew 1:18-20)

Do you think Joseph had planned to become a father at the age of 90?

Do you think Joseph had planned to marry a girl who shows up to the wedding with a baby in her tummy? A baby that clearly didn't belong to him?

Do you think Joseph had planned for any of this headache? Nope, nope, and nope. This was outside the plan . . . *WAY* outside the plan.

But Joseph goes with it . . . he goes with God's plan. He does exactly what God asks him to do and becomes the father to the most important Baby in the history of the world. He marries the Virgin Mary as he was instructed, and takes care of his new family as best he can. He trusts and obeys everything God tells him—even though it completely messes up *his* plan.

When all is said and done, Joseph has accomplished nothing of his original plan; every little box on the project plan is left unchecked. God has messed up everything and totally ruined Joseph's plan . . .

. . . And it was the best thing that ever happened to him!

TRADING MY PLAN FOR GOD'S PLAN

Like Joseph, God wants you to trade in your plans for His plans; He wants to ruin your plans just like He ruined Joseph's. For most of us, that's not an easy pill to swallow. We like our plans. Actually, we *love* our plans. We've worked hard on our plans and grown attached to them over the years. We count the days till we get to stop calling them *plans* and start calling them *REALITY*.

So why in the world should I be excited to trade my plan for God's plan? Two reasons:

1. God's plan is ALWAYS BIGGER than my plan.

Earlier we agreed that God is not like us. He doesn't think like us. He doesn't plan like us. He's nothing like us. Our hope is that we can one day be like Him, but He will never be like us. His ways are immeasurably higher than our ways, and His thoughts immeasurably higher than our thoughts.

Never is this more apparent than when it comes to making plans.

Joseph had a plan to serve God faithfully till the end of his life. He planned to be responsible for a wife and care for his family even in his old age. Good plan, right? Absolutely! In fact, God thought it was a good plan; He's the One who approved it. There wasn't anything wrong with the nature of the plan, but it was the *SIZE* of the plan that God wanted to change.

> Now to Him who is able to do exceedingly abun-
> dantly above all that we ask or think, according to
> the power that works in us. (Ephesians 3:20)

Did you hear that? *"Exceedingly abundantly above all that we ask or think"*! Other translations of this verse say, *"Immeasurably more than all we ask or imagine."*

That means that God—on His least creative, least imaginative, dullest day—is able to come up with plans that we—on our wildest, most creative, most imaginative, most inspired days—can't comprehend or even imagine. Even if you fed us brain food, gave us magical imagination pills, and quadrupled our brain capacity . . . we still wouldn't be anywhere near God's way of thinking! God is that much BIGGER!

That's because God sees things we can't see.

- We understand *facts*; God understands *possibilities*.
- We see what *is*; God envisions what *could be*.
- We use *past data* to plan for the future; God uses *limitless knowledge and foresight* to command the present.

Why? Because He's the God who *"is able to do exceedingly abundantly above all that we ask or think."* That's why!

Joseph thought, *"I'll take care of this young lady and she'll take care of me, and we'll live quietly ever after. That will be my faithful service to the Lord."*

God thought, *"Joseph, you're going to be the father of My Son!"*

God's plan is always bigger than my plan.

2. God's plan is INFINITELY BETTER than my plan.

Have you ever walked into an auto repair shop thinking that you were just coming for an oil change, only to walk out four hours later and realize that you just paid $1400 for a new transmission, four new tires, and a car wash?

You went in looking to receive *(and pay for)* something *small*, but you ended up getting something *BIG (and paying for it too).*

Well, in case you haven't already figured it out, God's plan will *never* be easier than our plan. It'll always be harder and require more sacrifice on our part. *(Just ask Joseph: retired life vs. changing diapers.)* And if we're honest, this is the reason we often resist it. It isn't always because we don't *BELIEVE* what He says; often, it's because we don't *LIKE* what He says.

For example:

> You therefore must endure hardship as a good soldier
> of Jesus Christ. (2 Timothy 2:3)

Verses like that don't make us excited to sign up for God's plan. Why choose *"hardship"* when I can settle for *"comfort"?* Why choose *"serve others"* when I can choose *"others serve me"?* Why choose *"giving"* when I'd rather choose *"receiving"?*

In other words, why should I choose God's plan instead of my own plan?

Simple. Because while it's true that God's plan will be *considerably HARDER* than your plan, I'll bet my life savings that it will also be *INFINITELY BETTER* than yours too.

> Eye has not seen, nor ear heard, nor have entered into the heart of man the things which God has prepared for those who love Him. (1 Corinthians 2:9)

Joseph couldn't have possibly imagined what would happen to him when he said yes to God's plan. In his wildest dreams, he couldn't have imagined a scenario where he would be given the honor to care for the Incarnate Son of God, to be Jesus's father on earth. Can you imagine what that was like?

We invite Jesus to bless our homes with His Presence. But Joseph never had to pray for that; he could just walk upstairs and get that blessing whenever he wanted.

We pray before our meals and invite Jesus to join us at our tables; Joseph had breakfast, lunch, and dinner with Jesus every single day.

We ask Jesus to hold us in His arms and keep us safe at night; Joseph got to hold little Baby Jesus in his arms and keep *Him* safe.

WOW! Who could have come up with *THAT* plan?! That truly is exceedingly, abundantly above all that we can ask for, or even imagine. And surely, no eye has seen nor ear heard, nor has come upon the heart of man the things which God has prepared for those who love Him, and for those who *TRUST* in His plan.

Joseph trusted and found out that God's plan was *bigger* and *better* than his own. Now it's your turn.

DON'T TRUST THE PLAN—TRUST THE GIVER OF THE PLAN

No matter where you are in life or what lies on your horizon, it's safe to say that one thing holds true for everyone reading this book: *God wants you to trust Him and trust His plan for your life.*

He doesn't want you to trust His plan because it makes more sense or because it's easier; He wants you to trust His plan because it's *HIS* plan. The goal isn't to trust the plan, but to trust the GIVER of the plan.

> But without faith it is impossible to please Him, for he who comes to God must believe that He is, and that He is a rewarder of those who diligently seek Him. (Hebrews 11:6)

Did you hear that? *"Without faith it is impossible to please him."* That means that no matter what you do—whether you fast or pray or give alms or memorize Scripture—no matter what you do, if you don't have faith, it is *IMPOSSIBLE* to please God.

Why is that? Think of it this way. As a father, what am I looking for from my children? What do I want from them when they're worried about their future?

"Dad, will we have food to eat tomorrow? Will we be able to afford new clothes when we get older? Will we run out of money and will a bad man come and take away our cable TV?" (#FirstWorldProblems)

What do I want from my son in that situation? How do I want him to respond? Would I be happy if he were to demand to see our monthly budget and bank statements? Would I be pleased if he says he needs me to provide him with a verification of employment so he's at ease about our expected income?

Of course not! I hope it never gets to that point. I don't *want* to do any of those things, and if I have to do them, then there's a major problem in our relationship.

I don't want him to trust *my plan*; I want him to trust *ME!* The giver of the plan! I don't want him to trust the plan because he understands it, but rather because I gave it.

If he can't trust me, then there's no way he can trust my plan. But if he can learn to trust me—his father and the provider of this household—it'll be that much easier for him to trust me when I "mess up" his plan later on down the road.

Why? Because in the end, it's not about trusting the plan; it's about trusting the giver of the plan.

> Those who trust in the Lord are like Mount Zion,
> which cannot be shaken but endures forever.
> (Psalm 125:1)

Trusting in God is one of the most powerful things that you'll ever do. It will open the door to endless possibilities for you. Had Joseph never trusted God, he could have lived a good life—but he certainly wouldn't have lived a *GREAT* life.

Your life's ceiling will be set by the level of trust you place in God. You'll never go higher than your level of trust.

With that said, it's time to get practical and learn how to increase our level of trust.

CHAPTER **14**

WHAT DO YOU GET WHEN YOU ADD 5 + 2?

*O*f all the commands in the Bible, which one's the hardest? You have plenty to choose from; the Bible's filled with laws and rules that we struggle to follow. So, which one is the most difficult to keep? The one that we struggle the most to obey?

Do not murder? Do not lie? Love your enemies? Turn the other cheek? Teenagers might say, *"Honor your father and mother."* If you're married you might vote for the commands in Ephesians 5: *"Husbands, love your wives"* and *"Wives, submit to your husbands."* You could easily make a case for *"Do not judge"* as well. But which is the hardest of them all?

Obviously, there's no "right answer," but there is *my answer*. And since I'm the writer and you're the reader, we'll just go ahead and assume that "my answer" and the "right answer" are interchangeable for now. Sound good?

I believe the hardest command is this:

> Be anxious for nothing, but in everything by prayer and supplication, with thanksgiving, let your requests be made known to God. (Philippians 4:6)

Did you catch that? Go back and read those first four words again: *"BE ANXIOUS FOR NOTHING."*

In other words, you're not supposed to worry about anything. Don't worry about your health. Don't worry about your kids. Don't worry about your job. Don't worry about the economy. Don't worry about the threat of terrorism. Even though it sounds like a complete impossibility, we are actually commanded to *"be anxious for nothing."*

In fact, this command is given to us more than once. Take a look at Jesus's most famous speech—called the Sermon on the Mount, where He gave all the major tenets of Christianity. Listen to what phrase He repeats three times in the middle of that speech:

> *"Therefore I say to you, DO NOT WORRY about your life,* what you will eat or what you will drink; nor about your body, what you will put on. Is not life more than food and the body more than clothing? . . .
> *"Therefore DO NOT WORRY,* saying, 'What shall we eat?' or 'What shall we drink?' or 'What shall we wear?' For after all these things the Gentiles seek. For your heavenly Father knows that you need all these things. But seek first the kingdom of God and His righteousness, and all these things shall be added to you.
> *"Therefore DO NOT WORRY about tomorrow,* for tomorrow will worry about its own things. Sufficient for the day is its own trouble." (Matthew 6:25, 31-34)

Usually when we think of Biblical commands, we think of big things, things that seem a lot more harmful than worrying. But not God. To Him, *"Do not worry"* is no different than

"Do not murder," or *"Do not steal,"* or *"Do not commit adultery."* They're at the same level. And *"Be anxious for nothing"* is equally as important as *"Be kind,"* and *"Be merciful,"* and *"Be patient."* In God's eyes, there's no difference. Each one is a command given to His children.

But is it even *possible* to live a worry-free life? Is that even attainable?

Who doesn't worry about their health? Every day we learn of something new that puts us at risk, and then we worry about how to avoid it.

Who doesn't worry about their friends and family? There's so much danger in the world today that anything can happen to anyone at any time—from drunk drivers to child abusers to school shooters.

Who doesn't worry about their financial security as they get older? With an economy that's up one day and down the next, it's almost impossible not to worry, isn't it?

And that's just the start. We haven't even gotten to the big worries, the stuff that affects us at a macro level, such as the environment, acts of terrorism, or the threat of war.

In the midst of all that, how can God tell us to *"be anxious for nothing?"* Is He serious?

WHY WORRY ABOUT WORRY?

First, let's understand the *reason* God commands us not to worry. If you don't know the *why* behind a command, you won't care as much about the *how*. Why does God care if we worry or not? Why does it matter to Him in the first place?

Let me ask you a different question: Why does a mother make rules for her children? Why does she say, *"You're not allowed to play in the street"?* What does it matter to her anyway? Is she doing it for own well-being? Of course not! A mother makes a rule for the sake of her children, not herself. It's in the children's best interests to obey, because when they do, they will be protected from danger. Rules are not made for the rule MAKERS; rules are made for the rule OBEYERS.

The same is true with God's command to *"be anxious for nothing."* God doesn't tell us not to worry because it's bad *for Him;* He tells us not to worry because it's bad *for us.* He isn't doing it for His well-being, but rather for ours.

We've known about the adverse physical effects of anxiety and stress for quite some time now. We know that if anxiety continues without relief, it can lead to a slew of health problems, such as chronic headaches, high blood pressure, heart problems, diabetes, skin conditions, asthma, arthritis, and depression. I even read once that between 75 to 80% of all doctor's office visits today are for stress or anxiety-related ailments.

In addition to the physical price, anxiety has a spiritual price as well. Worry is the opposite of trusting God. Think of worry and trust like two sides of a seesaw: when one side goes up, the other goes down. They are inversely proportional to each other. He who trusts much, worries little; he who trusts little, worries much.

And why does that matter? I said in the last chapter that *"Trusting in God is one of the most powerful things that you'll ever do . . . Your life's ceiling will be set by the level of trust you place in God. You'll never go higher than your level of trust."*

Worrying lowers your ceiling because it lowers your trust. It limits what God can/will do in your life. God may want to pour out rich blessings upon you, but your level of trust becomes the bottleneck that determines how much He pours in.

That's why God cares so much about our worries and anxieties. Like a good parent, He isn't commanding us not to worry for His sake, but for ours. He wants us to live up to the great potential He has planned for each one of us. And He knows that worry robs us of that potential.

> Blessed is the man who trusts in the Lord, and whose hope is the Lord. For he shall be like a tree planted by the waters, which spreads out its roots by the river, and will not fear when heat comes; but its leaf will be green, and will not be anxious in the year of drought, nor will cease from yielding fruit. (Jeremiah 17:7-8)

You can't be blessed if you don't trust, and you can't trust if you're worrying. That's why we need to get this *"worrying"* thing figured out.

A STRESSFUL SITUATION

Remember the story of Jesus with the five loaves and two fish? Let's go back and revisit that story, but from a different angle. This time, let's look at it from the perspective of Jesus's disciples, and see it from their sandals.

The story begins with the disciples just returning from a long trip. They'd been sent by Jesus to the neighboring towns to preach the gospel, cast out demons, and heal the sick in the Name of Jesus. Understandably, after returning from their trip, they were tired. *(You didn't think casting out demons was easy, did you?)*

They wanted to go to a quiet place together—away from the crowds—so they could share their experiences with Jesus and with each another.

But instead, they found themselves in the midst of a gigantic crowd: 5,000 men plus women and children. That would make the total number roughly 20,000 people. To put that number in perspective, that's more than the seating capacity in most professional basketball arenas in the United States. That's quite a lot of people! Not exactly what they had in mind for a nice, relaxing afternoon with Jesus.

But by this time, they had learned to expect the unexpected when they were with Jesus, so they went along with it, and were just waiting for the day to end so they could get their much-needed rest.

After spending all day preaching and doing miracles with the multitude, Jesus asked His disciples a strange question, the last question they were expecting and/or hoping to hear out of His mouth:

"Where shall we buy bread, that these may eat?" (John 6:5)

I would imagine that the disciples wanted to respond with something like this:

"What was that you said, Jesus? Where shall WE buy bread? Where did "we" come from? The proper question is where shall THEY buy bread. This isn't our problem; it's theirs. We can't solve it. There's nothing we can do about it, Jesus. It's bigger than us. Either You bring down some manna from heaven, or You let the people go and buy their own bread. Either way, there isn't much we can do here."

Jesus is making a crazy request. His disciples were exhausted. They had just come back from a long trip. The last thing they needed was to figure out the logistics of a dinner party with 20,000 of their closest friends. This was simply too much for them to handle.

I would imagine this request caused the disciples a bit of stress. Jesus was asking them to do something that was beyond their means, and the natural reaction would be worry and anxiety. That is seen clearly by the first response Jesus gets from Philip, His disciple:

> Philip answered Him, "Two hundred denarii worth
> of bread is not sufficient for them, that every one of
> them may have a little." (John 6:7)

You tell Him, Philip! Someone needs to be the voice of reason, and Philip was just that. He told Jesus that this request was beyond their resources and out of their league. Solid answer, Philip!

But another response comes in after Philip's, and this one is from the disciple Andrew:

> One of His disciples, Andrew, Simon Peter's brother,
> said to Him, "There is a lad here who has five barley
> loaves and two small fish, but what are they among
> so many?" (John 6:8-9)

This response may be even more crazy than Jesus's original request!

What do you mean that there's a lad here with five loaves and two fish? So what? What does that matter? We're talking about feeding 5,000 men plus women and children. Why would it matter if you have five loaves and two fish?

Imagine you just crashed your car and it requires $5,000 to repair. Then a friend comes over to your house and says, *"No problem, I have five nickels and two dimes. Here you go."*

Huh? What's that for? What's the use of five nickels and two dimes when you owe $5,000? The same question applies to Andrew. What's the use of five loaves and two fish if you need to feed 5,000 men? I could understand offering the five loaves and two fish if you were feeding five men instead of 5,000, but why in the world would Andrew make such an offer here?

I've come up with three options to explain Andrew's behavior:

a) He's not that smart and struggles with counting.
b) He thinks there's magic in those five pieces of bread and two pieces of fish *(which might make him eligible for option A as well)*.
c) He realizes that there's a special power in offering whatever you have—no matter how little it might be—into Jesus's hands.

Any guesses?

Andrew was no fool. He knew that what he was suggesting made no sense. He knew that logically, five loaves and two fish were of no value in this situation because the problem was so much bigger. But he offered it anyway; he did the opposite of what Philip did.

Philip focused on what he lacked (*"Two hundred denarii worth of bread is not sufficient for them"*), but Andrew focused on what he had (*"There is a lad here who has five barley loaves and two small fish"*).

And I'm pretty sure you know what happened next.

THE POWER OF OFFERING

There's a powerful lesson to be learned from what Andrew did. Some might read this story and see it as a story of God's power and what faith in God can do. Some would say that Andrew had more faith than Philip, and that he believed in Jesus more than Philip did.

I disagree 100%. I don't think this story is about faith at all. This isn't a story about how powerful Jesus is if we just believe in Him. I think Philip believed in Jesus just as much as Andrew did. Both disciples knew that Jesus was more than an ordinary man, and that He could do the miraculous in an instant if He wanted.

The difference between them wasn't their belief in the power of Jesus; the difference was their belief in *the power of their own personal offering*.

Philip thought, *"I have very little; it's not enough."* Andrew thought, *"I have very little; let me offer it to Jesus."* They didn't disagree on *Jesus's* role in making a miracle; they disagreed on their *own role* in making a miracle.

Let me see if I can put this in mathematical terms to make it clearer. There are three different ways of looking at what it takes to achieve the miraculous in your life.

Option One: 1 + 1 = 2

This is the approach that most people take (including Philip). No one would argue with it because it's logical and makes the most sense. This approach is based on the premise that *my resources should be equal to the problem I am trying to solve*.

Again, this is logical. You can't ask me to purchase a $5,000 item with only $500 in my pocket. If you want me to buy it, you have to give me more resources. If you don't, there's nothing I can do.

This is the approach which says if God gives me five pieces of bread, then God wants me to feed five people. No more, no less. If God wants me to feed more than five people, then He must give me more than five loaves—very simple and straightforward.

Your resources set the bar on what God wants from you because $1 + 1 = 2$.

Option Two: 0 + infinity = infinity

This misguided approach sounds very spiritual on the surface. This is the guy who says, *"I am nothing and God is everything. I trust that if He wants to feed all these people, He can turn these rocks into bread or bring food down from heaven like He did in the Old Testament."*

So far, so good. Nothing wrong yet. But the problem comes when that thinking leads to . . .

"So therefore, I'll just say a prayer and wish for the best. There's no reason for me to do anything; He doesn't need these pieces of bread and fish. He is God and I believe that all things are possible for Him."

This approach says that God has unlimited resources, so it doesn't really matter what I do. There's nothing you can add to infinity that makes any difference. Therefore, I will *do* nothing and let God do everything.

If option 1 was the logical choice, option 2 would be the ultra-spiritual choice. But neither of them is the right choice.

Option Three: 5 + 2 = 5000

This is the approach that Andrew took. He knew that God isn't limited to a "$1 + 1 = 2$" kind of a way. God is never limited by our lack of resources. But he also knew that God doesn't want us to sit around as passive observers and complain about the little that we have; instead, He wants us to *OFFER* the little that we have and trust that He will make something miraculous out of it.

Philip believed in option 1: *We can't do anything; our resources are limited.* The rest of the disciples believed in option 2: *We don't need to do anything; God is unlimited.* Andrew went with option 3: *On my own, my resources are not enough, but in the hands of God, anything is possible. I will offer my limited resources into the hands of an unlimited God and see what happens.*

Do you see the difference?

God doesn't want us to *limit* ourselves to only what we have in our hands, but He also doesn't want us to *neglect* what we have in our hands. He wants us to *OFFER* what we have into *His* hands.

Because when you place your limited resources into the hands of an unlimited God, miracles are going to happen.

OFFER RIGHT SACRIFICES AND TRUST IN THE LORD

I began this chapter speaking about the importance of decreasing our worry and increasing our trust. How do you do that? Simple—you follow the formula given in Psalm 4:5:

Offer right sacrifices and trust in the Lord. (Psalm 4:5)

In other words, do your best and trust God to do the rest.

"Offer right sacrifices" means you give God what you can; you offer what's in your hands. No matter how little or insignificant it may seem, you offer it because it's all you got; you do your best.

But then, after you've done your best, you invite God to work beyond your resources by *"trusting in the Lord."* You don't limit your expectations to just what's in your hands: You offer it in faith knowing that there's power in offering right sacrifices and trusting in the Lord. There's power in doing my best and trusting God to do the rest.

Once again, you know that when you place your limited resources into the hands of an unlimited God, miracles are going to happen.

What do you do if you're struggling financially and drowning in debt? *You offer right sacrifices and trust in the Lord.* Stop eating out. Stop going to the movies every weekend. Get a part-time job in the evenings and trust God to help you through it one day at a time.

What if you're feeling anxious about health issues? *You offer right sacrifices and trust in the Lord.* Start eating healthy, get plenty of exercise, and do your best to glorify God in your body. Also make time to invest in your spiritual health, knowing that it's connected to your physical health and neglecting either one will affect the other.

What do you do if you feel overwhelmed by the pressures of being a single mom? *You offer right sacrifices and trust in the Lord.* Pray for your family first and foremost, knowing that nothing gets results like prayer. Do your best to raise your children in the fear of God, and ask for help from your friends and family when you need it. You are not Superwoman *(even though you may feel like you need to be most of the time);* you need to realize your limitations. Do your best and trust God to do the rest.

"Offer right sacrifices and trust in the Lord." It's more than a nice verse — it's a way of life. It's about taking the little that's

in my hands and placing it faithfully into the BIG hands of God. It's about the power of offering. Don't tell me what you can't do; tell me what you have to offer.

Don't tell me that you don't have enough food to feed every homeless person. Do you have enough to feed just one? *Offer right sacrifices and trust in the Lord.*

Don't tell me that you can't pray without ceasing. Can you pray right now? *Offer right sacrifices and trust in the Lord.*

Don't tell me that you can't overcome your addiction. Can you fight to make it through this next hour or two without falling? *Offer right sacrifices and trust in the Lord.*

What will you choose to focus on the next time you feel stressed? Will you focus on what you lack (Philip)? Or will you focus on what you have (Andrew)? Will you stick to 1 + 1? Will you sit around and wait for 0 + infinity?

Or will you offer what little you have into the hands of the Almighty God and allow Him to show you how 5 + 2 = 5,000 in His book.

Your answer could mean the difference between witnessing a God-sized miracle or leaving hungry.

PART FOUR

GOD IS REWARDING

*A*t the start of this book, I said that my goal was to help you see that God is real, God is relevant, and God is rewarding. So far, we've covered the first two.

We first saw that God is REAL. He's a "He," not an "It." He's a Person who we can get to know and have a relationship with. Contrary to what many believe, God is not just some cosmic rule maker or law enforcer; He's not a tyrant who wants to control your life and take away your fun.

God is our Father. He's a GOOD Father, a GRACIOUS Father, and most of all, a very NEAR Father. And if you haven't yet experienced any of those traits, His greatest desire is to reveal them to you. Trust me, He wants to have a real Father-son or Father-daughter relationship with you, more than you'll ever know.

That's because God is real.

Then we saw that God is RELEVANT. In other words, He's much more than just a passive observer in your life. He is actively involved, every minute of every day. Just because we don't see it, doesn't mean that it isn't happening. We learned that God is always working behind the scenes of our lives to *"make all things work together for good to those who love Him."*

Therefore, no matter what happens to us, we can trust that God is in control. Even when circumstances get in the way of our plans, or people sabotage our plans, or even when God Himself "messes up" our plans, we know that He is still in full control and working all things together for good. He always finds a way to make something out of nothing, or to make 5,000 out of 5 + 2.

That's because God is relevant.

And now we get to the final and most needed section of this book, where we'll see that God is REWARDING.

Personally, this is the section that I'm most excited for you to read. Why? Because this is where so many books fall short. We hear a lot about what we're supposed to *do* as Christians and the *rules* we're supposed to follow. We hear a lot about what God wants *FROM* us, but we don't hear enough about what God wants *FOR* us.

Usually, when we think about "the reward" of a relationship with God, we think of heaven or life after death. Of course, that will be the absolute greatest reward ever—something unimaginable, which will last for all eternity.

But is that all? Or is there more? Didn't Jesus Himself promise another reward when He said:

> "Assuredly, I say to you, there is no one who has left house or brothers or sisters or father or mother or wife or children or lands, for My sake and the gospel's, who shall not receive a hundredfold *NOW IN THIS TIME*—houses and brothers and sisters and mothers and children and lands, with persecutions— and in the age to come, eternal life." (Mark 10:29-30)

Where is that *"now in this time"* reward? What is He talking about? Does He mean that we'll all be rich if we follow Him? *(I wish!)* Does He mean that we'll never have problems in our families? *(Yeah, right!)* Does He mean that the football team with the most Christians will always win the Super Bowl? *(You know someone who thinks that, don't you?)*

What's the *"reward"* that Jesus speaks about and how do we find it?

That's the goal of this fourth section: to see that God is not only real and relevant, but also REWARDING.

Any discussion about the *"reward"* of God cannot be had without discussing the most underappreciated aspect of God—the part of God that we rarely speak about because, in all honesty, we don't really understand.

What am I speaking about? Or rather *WHOM* am I speaking about? I'm speaking about the third Person of the Holy Trinity: the Comforter, the Helper, the Giver of Life, the Spirit of Truth, and the Spirit of God! I'm talking about the Holy Spirit—aka, the reward of God.

We first discovered that God is real through our relationship with Him as Father, a real Person that we can know and relate to. We then learned that He is relevant through His coming into our world and our lives through His Only Begotten Son, Jesus Christ. Now, we experience the true and lasting reward of being God's sons and daughters through our relationship with the Holy Spirit.

God is real (Father). God is relevant (Jesus His Son). God is rewarding (Holy Spirit).

The reason so many of us are living unsatisfied and unfulfilled lives—even though we think we're doing everything right on the outside—is because we miss out on this relationship with the Holy Spirit. We know the Father, and we speak often about the Son, but when it comes to the Holy Spirit, we find ourselves lacking. We don't really understand who the Holy Spirit is, and what role He plays in our lives.

Well, that's about to change. Say hello to your friendly neighborhood Paraclete.

Chapter 15

WHAT'S A PARACLETE?

"Nevertheless I tell you the truth. It is to your advantage that
I go away; for if I do not go away, the Helper (Paraclete)
will not come to you; but if I depart, I will send Him to you."
(John 16:7)

*T*hat's an incredible verse when you think about it. Do you
understand what Jesus is saying? Think about it from the
perspective of the disciples when they first heard it.

By this time, they had been following Jesus for three whole
years. They'd left their jobs, their homes, their friends and
family . . . they left everything to follow Jesus. Their only
job on a day-to-day basis was to follow Him and do whatever
He told them to do. He alone gave meaning and purpose to
their lives.

Death for Jesus meant orphanhood for the disciples. They
had nothing without Him. They were disciples and He was their
Master, and you can't be much of a disciple without a master.

So how could Jesus say that they'd be better off after He
left? How could that be true? Sure, it would be great to have
the Holy Spirit, but come on . . . this is JESUS we're talking

about! The five-loaves-and-two-fish Jesus. The walk-on-water Jesus. The healing-the-sick, casting-out-demons, raising-the-dead Jesus. Could it really be *"to your advantage"* for Him to go away? How could Jesus say that?

Clearly there's more here than meets the eye. Jesus must know something that we don't. What is it about the Holy Spirit that would lead Him to make such a bold claim?

Let's begin our discovery with a lesson in Greek.

THE PARACLETE:
NEVER LEAVE HOME WITHOUT HIM

The word *"Helper"* in the earlier verse comes from the Greek word *"parakletos,"* translated from the original Biblical text. From there, we get the little-used English word *"paraclete"* (PAR-uh-kleet or PAIR-uh-kleet).

What's a paraclete?

> *paraclete: an advocate, a helper, aider, assistant; one who pleads another's cause before a judge, a pleader*

The word in Greek literally means *"called to one's side."* A paraclete is someone who's on your side—someone advocating for you and pleading for you. He's someone who walks alongside you to assist in whatever way he can.

Imagine you're driving across the country and you have a paraclete with you, a helper to travel alongside you. What would he do? How would he assist you?

First, he'd check the map and give you the best directions. Then, he'd help you reroute when a road was closed, or if there was traffic, or if you simply missed the exit. If you were looking for a place to stop for food or gas, he'd know exactly where to go and how to get there. And if the road to get the food or gas was undergoing construction, he'd tell you where the potholes were and help you avoid them.

Not bad, huh? That's a paraclete. And there's more.

If you got distracted and started driving too fast, he'd remind you of the speed limit and tell you to slow down. And then—assuming you ignored him—he'd plead your case before the officer who pulled you over for speeding. And then—assuming *the officer ignored him*—your paraclete would find the money to bail you out of jail and book a motel for you to spend the night.

That's a paraclete! A helper. Someone to guide you, assist you, and plead your case.

And that's what we have in the Holy Spirit: a divine Paraclete! Someone to guide us when we're confused. Someone to assist us when we're overwhelmed. Someone to plead our case when we make mistakes.

That's what the Holy Spirit is to us. Or rather, that's *WHO* the Holy Spirit is to us. He's a Person—not in the physical sense, but in the same sense that God the Father is a Person, and His Son Jesus Christ is a Person as well. They are Persons in the sense that we can have a relationship with them. The Holy Spirit is also a Person who serves as our Paraclete, our Helper and our Advocate.

Now do you see why He's so valuable?

Jesus knew that we'd need help on this earthly journey and that we couldn't do it alone. He knew that we'd need guidance. We'd need instruction. We'd need someone to intercede for us and plead for us and advocate for us. If a journey across the country without a helper would be difficult, how much more difficult would it be to journey through this life without the Divine Paraclete?

> "I will pray the Father, and He will give you another Helper [Paraclete], that He may abide with you forever—the Spirit of truth, whom the world cannot receive, because it neither sees Him nor knows Him; but you know Him, for He dwells with you and will be in you. I will not leave you orphans; I will come to you." (John 14:16-18)

As much as the disciples benefited from living with their Master, the Lord Jesus, they had more to benefit from Him leaving and sending the Holy Spirit, the Paraclete, to them.

And that's saying quite a bit.

THE LESSON OF THE FELUCCA

Have you ever heard of a felucca? Probably not. It's an old, wooden sailboat that's still used in some parts of the world, especially along the Nile River in Egypt. They aren't the prettiest boats to look at, and they're certainly not the sturdiest, but they're quite popular among tourists looking for a relaxing, scenic ride along the Nile.

In 1996, I was one of those tourists. I went with my family on a two-week trip to Egypt. During our stay, we ventured out onto the Nile for a genuine felucca ride. What was supposed to be a nice, relaxing outing turned into an adventure that I'll never forget.

The felucca ride started out just fine. It was the five of us plus our felucca "engineer." He wasn't a real engineer, but that's just the title he gave himself. He was probably 65 to 70 years old and clearly not in the best physical condition. He could barely speak a sentence without coughing, and he struggled just getting the equipment into the boat without assistance.

It wasn't the most reassuring way to begin our outing, but what could happen? It's not like we were going across the Atlantic Ocean. It was supposed to be a 30-minute ride: fifteen minutes out from shore, make a U-turn, and then fifteen minutes back. What could go wrong?

I'll tell you what could go wrong . . . WIND! Or should I say . . . LACK of wind!

On the way out, things were fine. There was plenty of wind, and the felucca engineer successfully navigated the boat out to the halfway point of the trip. Then all of a sudden, seemingly in an instant, the wind stopped. It just stopped—out of nowhere. It was as if someone had pushed the "off" button and it just went away.

Thinking it was just a matter of minutes before it came back, we waited . . . and waited . . . and waited some more. Eventually we came to the unpleasant realization that it wasn't coming back and we needed to move on to plan B.

Now surely this kind of thing happens all the time, right? Obviously, a felucca engineer as "experienced" as this one had a backup plan—probably a small motor that he could attach to the boat to get us back safely. After all, he was an engineer, right?

Not exactly. Yes, he had a backup plan; but no, it wasn't a motor. The 70-year-old felucca engineer got up, limped his way to a big trunk at the back of the boat, and pulled out two wooden oars that looked even older than him!

"There's no way he's going to row us back to shore," I remember thinking. Are you kidding me? He could barely carry

the oars! Does he really think that he'll be able to row us all the way back on his own?

But that's exactly what he did . . . or at least, that's what he *tried* to do. We didn't get very far with him rowing. The poor guy tried his best, and he definitely got an "A" for effort, but he clearly wasn't up to the task physically.

Enter me and my brother with our *"I think I can, I think I can"* American bravado. *"Get of the way, Old Man! Here we come to save the day! Give us those oars!"*

I'll spare you the details and just say this: We did make it back safely that day, but not until my brother and I were about as physically exhausted as you should ever be allowed to be on vacation. It was much more taxing than I anticipated, and I think we'd still be out there today had the wind not kicked back in a little to help us get back to shore.

The sailing lesson I learned that day is this: Wind is more important than effort.

BIG MUSCLES + little wind = BIG EFFORT, *with little success*. Little muscles + BIG WIND = BIG SUCCESS, *with little effort*.

I wonder if there's a spiritual lesson there . . .

THE WIND TO YOUR FELUCCA

In describing the Holy Spirit, Jesus once said:

> "The wind blows where it wishes, and you hear the sound of it, but cannot tell where it comes from and where it goes. So is everyone who is born of the Spirit." (John 3:8)

The Holy Spirit—the Paraclete—is to your life what the wind was to that felucca. He makes everything work properly. When the Holy Spirit is present and active, things operate the way they are supposed to. You put in a little effort, and you get major results!

You stand to pray, and you feel God's Presence. You open your Bible, and you hear God's voice. You go to church, and you experience the love of God in community. That's how it's supposed to be! That's the reward of God! When the Holy Spirit is there, things work the way they are meant to work.

But without the Holy Spirit, the opposite is true. Nothing works right. Everything is tedious and tiresome and seems fruitless.

Without the Holy Spirit, prayer is lifeless. No matter how hard you struggle to concentrate and resist distraction, you just can't do it. You end up putting in lots of time and lots of effort with minimal results. No wind for your felucca.

Without the Holy Spirit, your Bible reading turns into nothing more than a history lesson, and your spiritual journal into a mere book report. You read the Bible hoping to hear God's voice, but you feel like you could hear a pin drop easier than the voice of God. You end up more confused than when you started. No wind for your felucca.

Without the Holy Spirit, church is nothing more than a country club—a gathering place for people of similar interests to share doughnuts and coffee. No power of God, no spiritual growth, no real community. No wind for your felucca.

In the church, we refer to the Holy Spirit as the *"Giver of Life."* He gives life to our spirit and to our spiritual activities: to our prayers and our Bible reading and our church gatherings. Without Him, our spiritual lives are dead; we're just going through the motions and following rules. But with Him, those same motions are full of energy, and those same rules lead to an abundant life.

He turns the *RULES OF* God into a *RELATIONSHIP WITH* God. That's His job. He's our Paraclete. He's the Giver of Life. It's time for us to stop living in ignorance when it comes to the Holy Spirit and His role in our lives. Jesus seemed to believe that the Holy Spirit could make a big difference for us; it's time for us to also believe it and find out how.

In the next three chapters, we'll look at three of the ways that the Holy Spirit acts in our day-to-day lives. We'll see that:

a) When He guides, He provides.
b) When He corrects, He protects.
c) When He works, the ordinary becomes extraordinary.

Obviously, He does a lot more than this, but we'll use these three as starting points. From there, hopefully we can begin to develop a relationship with the Holy Spirit and discover even more of what He brings into our lives—knowing that a relationship with Him is the key to experiencing the true "reward" of being the sons and daughters of God.

"If you then, being evil, know how to give good gifts to your children, how much more will your heavenly Father give the Holy Spirit to those who ask Him!" (Luke 11:13)

CHAPTER 16

WHEN HE GUIDES, HE PROVIDES

*W*ho remembers MapQuest? Come on you forty-some-
things out there . . . don't leave me hanging here. When
it first came out, we thought MapQuest was the greatest inven-
tion of all time! It told you everything you needed to know
to drive to any place on the planet—which road to take, how
long to stay on it, when to turn, etc. All you had to do was tell
it your starting point, and where you wanted to end up, and
that was it! Voila! It took care of all the details. Driving would
never be the same again! And obviously that was just the beginning. Nowadays most everyone has a navigation system, which
makes using MapQuest to drive feel like using a compass to
fly a plane!

But do you remember life *before* MapQuest? *(I know I'm
dating myself.)* Do you remember when we used to use those
crazy old things called maps?

In theory, a map could do everything MapQuest or your
GPS could do. It could provide you with the same information
and even more. But the problem was that a map relied heavily
on your ability to process that information and turn it into an
action plan on your own.

You needed to understand that the fastest distance between two points wasn't always a straight line. Sometimes you needed to choose the longer route because it would be faster. You also needed to know that you didn't always have to go north to get north; sometimes you'd actually want to go south to get north, or north to get south.

And maps wouldn't tell you about road closures or one-way streets. They wouldn't warn you if there was traffic or a major accident. Maps just provided you with general information, and it was up to you to put it all together and figure out what to do next.

Compare that to a GPS, which gives you turn-by-turn navigation, and warns you when there's a traffic jam, or an accident, or an unexpected road closure. No comparison!

Maps are good, but a GPS is better. Maps give you options, but a GPS gives you steps. Maps give you general information, but a GPS gives you a personalized plan.

YOUR PERSONAL GPS

In the same way that using a GPS has revolutionized our ability to navigate from one place to another, developing a relationship with the Holy Spirit will revolutionize your ability to navigate through this life and into the next.

> "When He, the Spirit of truth, has come, He will guide you into all truth; for He will not speak on His own authority, but whatever He hears He will speak; and He will tell you things to come." (John 16:13)

The Holy Spirit—our Paraclete, our Helper—also happens to be our *GUIDE*. He's our personal GPS. He knows where we are today and where we need to go tomorrow, and He's ready to give turn-by-turn directions if we let Him.

Just as a GPS takes information from a map and personalizes it for your specific journey, the Holy Spirit does the same with the teachings in the Scriptures. He personalizes it for your specific circumstance. He takes the laws, the commandments, and everything else in there, and breaks it down into customized steps for each of us.

For example, a map tells you that you need to go west to reach your destination. But a GPS tells you to take Route 50 West for 12 miles, then take Exit 19, and turn right onto Johnson Street. The map gives the general plan, but the GPS provides the details.

In the New Testament, Jesus taught that we should love our enemies. But the Holy Spirit is the One who translates that to specific action steps. He tells you to go to your estranged brother and apologize. He tells you to stop gossiping about your boss behind her back. He tells you to let go of the grudge that you've been holding onto for years.

In the Old Testament, it says, *"Do not commit adultery."* But the Holy Spirit is the One who tells you to stop flirting with your co-worker. Or He tells you to get an internet filter for your computer. Or He tells you to stay away from those trashy novels that you like to read on the beach.

Do you see how He works? Like a GPS, the Holy Spirit gives us a personalized path to reach our destination. Without Him, traveling wouldn't be the same. We'd still be able to read the Bible, and maybe even understand it at times, but without Him, we'd really struggle to know how to *APPLY IT* to our lives. He makes it personal.

Before there was MapQuest and before there was GPS, driving to new places was difficult. But now that we have these tools, it's become a lot easier. No more maps. No more stopping to ask for directions. No more guessing which street to turn on and then hoping for the best. We now have tools *alongside* us to *help us* to reach our destination. We no longer have to rely solely on ourselves; now we have a guide.

The same is true spiritually. We've been given the gift of the Holy Spirit—our Guide, our Helper, our Paraclete. He's with us and His first role is to guide us, from wherever we stand today, into the Kingdom of God. We don't need to travel alone. We don't need to rely on others for directions. We don't need to just guess and hope for the best. We now have the Paraclete alongside us.

Easy, right?

Uh . . . not exactly . . . are you going to tell me how to HEAR the Holy Spirit? I know how to turn on the GPS in my car, but is there an ON/OFF switch for the Holy Spirit? How do I know if He's working? And is there a volume button? If so, I think we may need to turn it up. How do I make sure that I can hear His voice?

I'm glad you asked.

LEARNING TO HEAR HIS VOICE

Imagine a crowded room, filled with 25 women—one of whom happens to be my wife. As we enter, the women are all conversing simultaneously. All you hear is a jumbled assortment of voices.

Do you think you'd be able to recognize which voice belongs to my wife? *Probably not.* Do you think I could? *Probably, yes.*

Why is that? How come you couldn't tell which voice was hers but I could?

Two reasons: You either a) don't know my wife, or b) don't spend much time talking with her. If either of these scenarios is true, you'd have a difficult time trying to separate her voice from among so many.

Back to the Holy Spirit. How can I distinguish His voice from all the other voices around me and in my head? How do I know what He is saying to me?

Same as above. First, you have to know Him. Second, you have to spend time talking with Him.

First, you have to know Him.

In other words, you must begin a relationship with Him. Too many of us think of the Holy Spirit as some kind of Magic 8-Ball or a fortune cookie. We see Him as a God-approved version of the psychic hotline. *"Hi, my name is Billy Ray, and I want to know if I should take this job and marry this girl, OR take that job and marry that girl? Which is it? Please guide me, Holy Spirit. Ready . . . set . . . GUIDE!"*

That's not how it works.

In this regard, the Holy Spirit is less like a GPS *(impersonal, just shouts instructions)* and more like a primary care physician: a person who wants to get to know you, and establish a relationship with you, and be involved in the details of your life.

It's through this relationship that He gives specific guidance for our unique circumstances. His instructions are like personalized prescriptions—tailor-made just for us and for our situation. He gives us exactly what we need, exactly when we need it.

But to receive this *personalized* guidance, we need to get *personal* with the Holy Spirit. We need to open up specific areas of our lives, and ask for His guidance in those areas—areas such as our thought patterns, our habits, our careers, our relationships, our finances, our fears and anxieties, our hopes, and our dreams.

Like a doctor, He can't heal what we don't expose. He can't enter what we don't open. He can't lead where He's not invited.

He'll only guide those areas where we say, *"God, I want to do Your will and obey Your command in this area of my life. Please be my guide and lead me to the path that leads to Your Kingdom."*

There's no guidance without relationship.

Second, you have to spend time talking with Him.

Knowing God is good—that's the starting point. But there's more. The relationship develops as we communicate with one another more and more.

Today I can discern my wife's voice because I've spent 16 years talking with her about anything and everything. We talk about our finances and about our kids. We talk about our dreams and about our fears. We talk about what makes us laugh and about what makes us scared. We once even talked about what superpower we'd choose if we were ever given the choice. *(It's always good to be prepared.)*

We talk and talk and talk. I have the green light to talk to her about *anything,* and she has the same green light with me. Nothing is off limits.

And because of all that talking, I can recognize her voice, even when other voices are competing for my attention. I wouldn't have been able to say this when we first married, but today—after 16 years of talking—I'm confident I could walk into that room of 25 women, *blindfolded,* and pick out her voice in seconds.

Why? Because a) I know my wife, and b) I spend plenty of time talking with her.

In the same way, you can get better at hearing God's voice too. Anybody can. No experience necessary.

"My sheep hear My voice, and I know them, and they follow Me." (John 10:27)

According to Jesus, hearing the Shepherd's voice is a defining characteristic of being of His sheep. It's what turns *A* sheep into *HIS* sheep; it's what makes us His.

But you can't separate *"hear my voice"* from *"I know them."* One requires the other. That's because hearing God's voice isn't about a formula to adopt or a blueprint to follow; there's no secret handshake or special code words you need to memorize. It's not about following a prescribed set of rules, but rather it's about cultivating a relationship.

And as with any relationship, the way you deepen it is by regular communication, and communication takes PRACTICE!

Practice talking to God in prayer. Practice listening to God through Scripture. Practice saying, *"I love you, God,"* by loving your neighbor. Practice hearing Him say, *"I love you back,"* through fellowship at your local church.

Practice, practice, practice. Nothing valuable comes without practice—and that includes the ability to discern God's voice.

So forget about formulas. Stop looking for gimmicks to get answers. Focus on cultivating your relationship with the Holy Spirit through regular communication, and trust that He WILL BE speaking.

How? Sometimes He'll speak through prayer, and other times He'll speak through a sermon. Sometimes He'll speak through the Bible, and other times He'll speak through a random email or text message from a friend. He can speak through circumstances, through books, through gut feelings, through phone calls with your mother, through songs on the radio, and in a thousand other ways that we can't even imagine!

Like my wife, there's no limit to the number of ways that the Holy Spirit can communicate to us, IF WE ARE WILLING TO LISTEN.

The question isn't *"will He speak?"* The question is *"will you be able to hear Him when He does?"* Will you have spent enough time with Him—practicing talking and listening—to be able to discern His voice?

Only you can answer that one.

THE RESULT OF HIS GUIDANCE

One of the most well-known passages of Scripture comes from Psalm 23. Here David shows us where the Holy Spirit's guidance will lead us if we follow it:

> The Lord is my shepherd; I shall not want. He makes me to lie down in green pastures; He leads me beside the still waters. He restores my soul; He leads me in the paths of righteousness for His name's sake.
>
> Yea, though I walk through the valley of the shadow of death, I will fear no evil; for You are with me; Your rod and Your staff, they comfort me. You prepare a table before me in the presence of my enemies; You anoint my head with oil; my cup runs over.
>
> Surely goodness and mercy shall follow me all the days of my life; and I will dwell in the house of the Lord forever." (Psalm 23)

My favorite part is the first line, *"The Lord is my shepherd, I shall not want."*

That's what happens when you allow the Holy Spirit to guide you and follow the path He lays out—when you allow Him to be your shepherd. You'll end up saying, *"I shall not want."* In other words, *"I'm perfectly content. I have everything I need. There is nothing that I lack or desire."*

But you'll never be able to say, *"I shall not want,"* until you're first ready to say, *"The Lord is my shepherd."* One is the direct result of the other.

Why? Because when He GUIDES, He PROVIDES.

He knows exactly what you need. He knows where you are and where you need to be. And He's got the perfect plan to get you there. *(Remember the GPS?)* But the key will be your ability to know Him and to hear His voice.

This might be another one of those moments where you'll want to bow your head and say a prayer. Ask the Holy Spirit to fill your heart with His Presence and help you better discern His voice. Tell Him that you want Him to guide your life, and that you're ready to listen. Tell Him whatever's in your heart because that's how you develop a relationship with someone—by talking to them.

And if it helps, here is an ancient prayer written specifically to the Holy Spirit that can help you get started:

"O Heavenly King, the Comforter, the Spirit of Truth, who is present everywhere, and fills all. You are the Treasury of Goodness and Giver of Life graciously come and dwell within us, purify us of every iniquity, O Good One, and save our souls."

CHAPTER 17

WHEN HE CORRECTS, HE PROTECTS

*G*rowing up, we all knew at least one kid who was allowed to do whatever he wanted. No rules. No curfews. No list of TV shows that he couldn't watch. There was always that one kid whose parents seemed to let him do whatever he wanted.

For me, that was "Joey Berryville" *(name changed in case the real Joey Berryville or his parents ever read this)*. Joey and I went to the same elementary school and middle school, and were good friends for most of that time. Joey was the youngest of five brothers, and that meant he pretty much got to do whatever he wanted.

Back in the day (late 1980s), all of us guys wanted to grow our hair long, like the guys from Guns N' Roses, Def Leppard, and Mötley Crüe ('80s rock stars). But there was only one kid whose parents actually let him do it. Who? Joey Berryville.

When we wanted to see a PG-13 movie, and we knew none of our parents would let us go, whose house would we go to? Joey Berryville's house. His parents would take us to the theater and buy us tickets, without even asking what the movie was rated.

On Halloween night, during the annual town parade, we would all beg our parents to extend our curfews as late as possible. But who was always the last to leave? Yep, Joey Berryville. He actually had a curfew, but somehow it never seemed to matter if he broke it or not!

Joey Berryville pretty much got away with whatever he wanted. To this day, I don't allow my son to go to sleepovers because of the stuff we used to sneak out and do when we spent the night at Joey's house.

From where we were standing back in middle school, Joey Berryville was living the good life.

Or was he?

At the time, we all envied Joey. We wished our parents would let us do the things he was allowed to do. We wished they would be as "cool" as Joey's parents and not make such a big deal out of how late we stayed out, or what movies we watched, or what we did with our friends after school. But as we grew older and more mature, our perspective changed.

I no longer envy the Joey Berryvilles of the world. They may have had fun in middle school, but they missed out on something extremely valuable in life—something you can't put a price tag on.

They missed out on parental CORRECTION.

> My son, do not despise the chastening of the Lord, nor detest His correction; for whom the Lord loves He corrects, just as a father the son in whom he delights. (Proverbs 3:11-12)

Whether a child realizes it or not, correction is one of the greatest gifts that can be given to them by a loving parent. Children need boundaries to protect them, and they need correction when they step outside of those boundaries. It's vital to growing up and maturing.

In the same way, receiving correction from the Holy Spirit is one of the greatest "rewards" of having God as our Father. It may not always seem like it at the time, but the Holy Spirit's correction is instrumental in making us who we were meant to be. Without it, we're lacking an essential component for our growth and maturity.

How does that work? What does that correction look like?

FINDING COMFORT IN THE SHEPHERD'S ROD

In the last chapter, we talked about how the Holy Spirit guides us, and we looked at a passage from Psalm 23. We saw that the one who says, *"The Lord is my shepherd,"* will also be the one who can say, *"I shall not want."*

But there's another lesson we can learn from this as well. In speaking about the Lord as his shepherd, David says, *"Your rod and Your staff, they comfort me." (Psalm 23:4)*

A shepherd always has two instruments at his disposal while doing his job: a staff and a rod. Each item is essential; each serves a purpose.

Let's start with the staff. What do you think it's used for?

The staff is for *GUIDANCE*—that's what we saw in the last chapter. The Holy Spirit is our guide; He points us in the direction that He knows is best for us. We open up our lives to Him, and He guides us to the path that leads to satisfaction and refreshment. As a shepherd lifts his staff high so that all his sheep can see it and follow, the Holy Spirit finds a way to make His guidance known to the one who opens up his or her life to Him.

That's the staff; it's used for guidance.

So how about the rod? What's that used for? The name alone suggests that it isn't going to be something that I like.

The rod is for *CORRECTION*. It was used to discipline the sheep when they went astray. I know it sounds cruel, but the shepherd would use the rod to strike the sheep that had wandered off or ignored the guidance of his staff. And if a certain sheep was a repeat offender—one that had a habit of wandering off—the shepherd would hit the sheep so hard, it would leave the sheep injured for a short time and unable to walk without a limp.

That doesn't sound very fun! Why would David—a shepherd by trade who knows exactly how much pain a rod can inflict upon a sheep—say, *"Your rod and your staff they comfort me"?* I understand why the staff is comforting, but the *ROD?* How is there comfort in that?

There are three facts we need to understand about how the "rod of correction" works—both with a shepherd and also with the Holy Spirit.

1. *The motivation is DISCIPLINE, not punishment.*

The shepherd doesn't use his rod to *punish* his sheep for straying; he uses the rod to *discipline* them so they learn not to stray again. What's the difference?

Punishment focuses on the past; discipline focuses on the future. Punishment chastises you for what you did; discipline corrects you to help you avoid doing it again. Punishment seeks to cause *pain;* discipline seeks to cause *change*.

What happens to sheep when they stray from the shepherd and from the flock? What happens when they're on their own?

What do they do when they face a predator out in the wild? How do they protect themselves?

Some animals defend themselves by attacking, some by running, some by outsmarting their opponent, some by hiding. But sheep can do none of those things. They don't have any offensive weapons for fighting: no fangs, no claws, no horns, no stingers. They don't have any defensive weapons to protect themselves—like the shell of a turtle or the ability of a chameleon to change colors. Sheep certainly can't outrun many animals, and they're even less likely to be able to outsmart one.

They aren't strong and they aren't fast. They can't fight and they can't run. They can't even try to scare you away with a bark, or even a meow. Sheep are about as defenseless as it gets!

And a shepherd knows that.

A shepherd knows that allowing a sheep to wander off means allowing that sheep to be killed. The sheep may not realize it, but the shepherd does, and that's why it's critical for him to teach his sheep this lesson by whatever means necessary.

So injuring the sheep temporarily, and rendering it unable to stray might not be such a bad thing after all. Like a teenager having his driver's license revoked until he's responsible enough to drive, the sheep may not like it at the time, but that injury may end up saving the sheep's life.

The sheep's inability to comprehend the value of the correction doesn't stop the shepherd from doing what's best for the sheep. As a good shepherd, he uses whatever means he can to teach his sheep to stay safe, even if that means hurting them at times.

His motivation is discipline, not punishment.

2. The aim is HEALING, not harm.

Listen to what the prophet Job says about the correction of the Lord:

> Behold, happy is the man whom God corrects; there-
> fore do not despise the chastening of the Almighty.
> For He bruises, but He binds up; He wounds, but
> His hands make whole. (Job 5:17-18)

Did you catch that? *He bruises, but He binds up. He wounds, but His hands make whole.*

I mentioned earlier that when the shepherd uses his rod, it often leaves the sheep injured and unable to walk for a short time. So, then what? How does this help the sheep? Yeah, the sheep learns not to wander off, but now it's unable to keep up with the rest of the flock! Wouldn't that make it even *more* of a target for predators?

This is where the true love and motivation of the shepherd is seen. Yes, he bruises, but He also binds up. Yes, He wounds, but His hands also make whole.

The shepherd doesn't leave the injured sheep; he places the wounded animal upon his shoulders and carries it until it is healed. He knows that the wounded sheep is in GREATER NEED than the others, and therefore he gives it special attention until it is ready to rejoin the flock. Not only will this give the sheep time to rest and heal from its injury, but there's another objective that the shepherd is aiming for as well.

By placing the sheep upon his shoulders, the shepherd ensures that the wounded animal—that became wounded because it disobeyed or ignored the shepherd's instructions—can be close to the shepherd at all times. And not just close to the shepherd's body, but specifically close to his mouth . . . to hear his voice.

While the sheep is being carried on the shepherd's shoulders, it will hear the shepherd's voice all day long—calling out commands, instructing the sheep, and guiding them to safety. The sheep will come to recognize that voice as one of comfort and protection, and not one of fear and punishment.

In other words, the shepherd isn't just trying to solve a short-term problem *(leg is injured);* he is attempting to solve a long-term problem as well *(sheep doesn't recognize/trust my voice).*

> Behold, happy is the man whom God corrects; therefore do not despise the chastening of the Almighty. For He bruises, but He binds up; He wounds, but His hands make whole. (Job 5:17-18)

Correction aims for healing, not harm.

3. The same rod of correction is also the rod of PROTECTION.

"That's it, we've had enough," say the sheep one day. *"We can't take that shepherd and his rod anymore. We've had enough! Every time we try to have a little fun around here by wandering off into the wilderness, he uses that dumb rod to knock us back in line. No more! It's time for us to take back our freedom and GET RID of that rod!"*

I can't say for sure that's how a sheep thinks, but I'm pretty sure that's what you and I would be thinking if we were in their place. Human beings don't like being told what to do. We don't like taking orders. We don't like feeling like someone is taking away our ability to choose for ourselves. And when we do feel that way, it's only a matter of time before we revolt!

So, let's assume that the sheep in this story think like us, and that the prior monologue is true. Let's assume that the sheep are sick and tired of being told what to do, and they have decided to take action! They will revolt!

"All right guys, today is the day," says Curly, the leader of the sheep revolt. *"Lambchop, you cause a diversion. Lambo, you go in and steal the rod. Without the rod, the shepherd will be powerless against us, and we'll show him who's boss around here!"*

After a surprisingly flawless execution, the sheep succeed in securing the shepherd's rod. They've disarmed the shepherd and taken away his only weapon. The shepherd is powerless against them.

This is perfect! Too good to be true. What could go wrong?

Cue the wolf.

The wolf does what a wolf does; he jumps the fence and attacks sheep. But that's okay. This isn't anything unusual. Wolves attack sheep all the time. As long as the shepherd is nearby, it shouldn't be a problem. The wolf may get close, but he's no match for the shepherd. The shepherd knows how to protect his sheep. He is trained in how to fight off the wolf. This should be a piece of cake for him . . .

All he needs is his rod.

"Uh-oh," thinks Lambo. *"Maybe we shouldn't have thrown that rod into the river after all . . ."*

The same rod the shepherd uses to *CORRECT* his sheep, is also the rod he uses to *PROTECT* his sheep. It's not just the rod of correction, it's also the rod of protection. And without that rod, *WE* are the ones who lose.

HOW DOES GOD CORRECT US?

It's easy to see how a shepherd corrects his sheep, and why sheep need correction, but how does God correct us? He doesn't hit us with a stick like a shepherd, does He?

Maybe He uses natural disasters like hurricanes and earthquakes and tsunamis. Is that the correction of God?

Or maybe He gives us diseases and epidemics—like cancer or HIV—to teach us a lesson?

Or maybe He uses wicked people—like Hitler or Stalin or insert your (least) favorite dictator here? Maybe God uses them to humble us when we do bad things?

Or maybe He keeps it simple and just ruins our lives by causing us to lose our jobs, struggle relationally, and never find true satisfaction in life?

Is that how God works?

Keeping in mind the three principles of the shepherd's rod (discipline not punishment, healing not harm, correction plus protection), the answer isn't any of the above. So, what is it, then? How does God correct His children?

Unfortunately, I can't say for sure. I can't give you a formula that God follows every time He corrects us. Remember, God is a Person, not a robot. And our life with God is a relationship, not a science. So I can't tell you exactly how God will correct you, but I know that He'll find a way:

- It could be through a sermon you hear on Sunday . . .
- It could be through a conversation with your mother . . .
- It could be through a not-quite-right feeling in your heart while you're praying . . .
- It could be through a dream in the middle of the night . . .

- It could even be through the book that's in your hands right now . . .

I don't know how . . . and I don't know when . . . and I don't know what it'll look like . . . but I guarantee you that if you're truly seeking to live the life that pleases God, HE WILL FIND A WAY. A good father always finds a way to correct his children and get them back on track when they've gone astray.

Earlier I said that the Holy Spirit is like your own personal GPS. He guides you through all the twists and turns that life throws at you. What does a GPS do when you make a wrong turn? When you disobey its command—either intentionally or unintentionally?

Will it give up on you and say, *"I've had it with this driver!"?* Will it leave you to drive off into oblivion, knowing that you're going the wrong direction?

Of course not! It will say what it's programmed to say, *"REROUTING."* And if you're like me and think you're smarter than the GPS, and like to prove it by going against its instructions, you know that there's NO LIMIT to the number of times that it will reroute you until you get to your destination.

Like that GPS, there's no limit to how many times the Holy Spirit will lovingly and kindly correct us when we go astray. Once we decide that we want to live with God, and for God, the Holy Spirit goes to work.

> "I will send Him (Holy Spirit) to you. And when He
> has come, He will convict the world of sin, and of
> righteousness, and of judgment . . ." (John 16:7-8)

"Convict" sounds like a scary word, but it's not. It's not scary when I know that the one doing the convicting is trying to help me, not hurt me . . . to heal me, not harm me . . . to protect me, not just correct me.

It's not a scary word when I trust the one doing the convicting.

And why should I trust Him? On to the next chapter . . .

CHAPTER 18

WHEN HE WORKS, THE ORDINARY BECOMES EXTRAORDINARY

*R*emember a few chapters ago when I shared my experience on the felucca? Remember how frustrating it was when the wind just stopped and we were stuck out in the middle of the river? Remember how we started the felucca ride, expecting one thing—a relaxing trip along the Nile, but then finished the ride feeling the exact opposite: tired, exhausted, and drained?

What if that wasn't just a one-time experience? What if that was your daily life? What if you were a felucca engineer and that was how you lived every day? Out on the water with no wind, struggling to paddle your way home . . .

Imagine that you see a documentary portraying the thrill of sailing rickety old boats in the Middle East, and then you decide that driving a felucca is now your calling. *"It's time to start living the good life,"* you think to yourself. Enough with the boring desk job and nine-to-five lifestyle. You want adventure. You want excitement. You want to be a felucca engineer!

But then similar to my felucca experience, every time you get out there, there's a problem . . . NO WIND! You discover that the felucca isn't as much fun without wind. You spend the entire day out in the boat, but instead of finding fun and adventure, all you come home with is frustration and exhaustion. This isn't what you signed up for.

Day after day, you venture out onto the water with optimism and enthusiasm, expecting that "today will be different." But much to your chagrin, the wind never comes. You start every day optimistically (*"This will be the day when it all comes together"*), only to return at the end of each day disheartened (*"Why am I doing this again?"*).

With each day that passes, you come home a little more frustrated and a little more exhausted.

How long do you think you could keep this up? How long would it be until you said, *"Enough is enough"?* This clearly isn't what you were expecting when you quit your job and moved to Egypt. You were expecting fun and adventure, but so far, there's been nothing but disappointment and discouragement.

How long can you continue to do something when you aren't experiencing the results you were promised?

Jesus once said:

> "I have come that they may have life, and that they
> may have it more abundantly." (John 10:10)

If you've been a Christian for any significant amount of time, I bet you've either heard a sermon or read a book based on that verse. That verse has inspired preachers, authors, and Christians everywhere to speak about *"the abundant life"* that God desires to give us all. A life full of joy. A life full of peace.

A life full of power. God's children aren't supposed to be living defeated and discouraged like everyone else; we're supposed to have something better.

Or at least, that's what we've been told. That's why we signed up for this *"relationship with God"* thing—we did it because we thought it would make our lives better. We thought it would give us peace and hope and joy, and all kinds of good stuff like that.

But more often than not, the promise of an abundant life goes unrealized. It sure sounds nice in a sermon, or looks impressive in a book, but when it comes time for reality, it seems like they're just empty words—like a sales pitch to get people to become Christian. *"Follow Jesus and we'll throw in the ABUNDANT life as well."*

Is that really just a sales pitch? Or am I missing something here? Jesus did promise an abundant life, didn't He? Well, where is it?

Why is my life full of so much confusion, even though I pray for guidance every day? Why can't I get past this hurt or this addiction that I've been struggling with for so long? How come no matter what I do, I can't seem to stop messing up my relationships?

Where is this "abundant life," God?

If you've ever felt like you're living a less-than-abundant life, I have good news for you . . . I HAVE A SOLUTION. I know where you can find that abundant life and start claiming it as your own. I know how you can get some wind for your felucca.

It's simple. Just order some wine.

WHEN THE WINE RUNS DRY

One of my favorite passages from all of Scripture comes from John 2. It's the story of when Jesus performed His very first public miracle at a wedding in a city called Cana.

> On the third day, there was a wedding in Cana of Galilee, and the mother of Jesus was there. Now both Jesus and His disciples were invited to the wedding. And when they ran out of wine, the mother of Jesus said to Him, "They have no wine."
>
> Jesus said to her, "Woman, what does your concern have to do with Me? My hour has not yet come."
>
> His mother said to the servants, "Whatever He says to you, do it."
>
> Now there were set there six waterpots of stone, according to the manner of purification of the Jews, containing twenty or thirty gallons apiece. Jesus said to them, "Fill the waterpots with water." And they filled them up to the brim. And He said to them, "Draw some out now, and take it to the master of the feast." And they took it.
>
> When the master of the feast had tasted the water that was made wine, and did not know where it came from (but the servants who had drawn the water knew), the master of the feast called the bridegroom. And he said to him, "Every man at the beginning sets out the good wine, and when the guests have well drunk, then the inferior. You have kept the good wine until now!"
>
> This beginning of signs Jesus did in Cana of Galilee, and manifested His glory; and His disciples believed in Him." (John 2:1-11)

I've always wondered why this is the *first* miracle that Jesus decided to do. Kinda strange, don't you think? His first miracle wasn't healing a sick person or casting out a demon. He didn't start with a big splash, like feeding the five thousand or moving a mountain.

His first public miracle was making sure that a wedding reception had enough wine for people to drink. And not just any wine, but apparently—based on the last couple of verses in the story—when Jesus is responsible for the wine at a party, He brings the good stuff!

How can *this* be Jesus's first miracle? What's so special about turning water into wine?

I believe this miracle is a microcosm of our life with God. It shows exactly what He wants to do in each of our lives—if we just let Him. And that is this:

He wants to transform the *NATURAL* into the *SUPERNATURAL* . . . the *ROUTINE* into the *REMARKABLE* . . . the *ORDINARY* into the *EXTRAORDINARY*.

In other words, He wants to take the water in your life and turn it into wine.

Let me explain.

To fully appreciate this story, you have to understand how weddings were celebrated back in Jesus's day. Things were quite different than they are today; those guys really knew how to party!

Back then, weddings weren't just single-day events; they were more like festivals. They lasted at least three days, and sometimes up to a full week! People didn't go on honeymoons back then; so instead, weddings would just be one long party—with guests coming and going throughout the week as they pleased.

And when the guests arrived, THERE HAD TO BE WINE! It wouldn't be a feast otherwise.[2] According to Jewish custom, running out of wine would be a major faux pas.

Think of it like running out of cake at your birthday party in second grade . . . a major disgrace to say the least!

So here they are at the wedding of Cana, a house full of guests expecting to drink wine, but there's none—only water. The wine has run dry, and the party is about to die.

But that's when Jesus steps onto the scene and changes everything. He performs His very first miracle. He takes the water and *transforms* it into wine. He gives new life and new taste to the celebration, and teaches us an important lesson in the process.

WHAT'S WATER? AND WHAT'S WINE?

What's the wine and what's the water in this story? What does each represent? Obviously, this is more than just a lesson in oenology. *(Oenology is a new word I just learned; it means "the science and study of wine." You really can find everything on Wikipedia.)*

What's water? And what's wine?

- Water is plain; wine is special.
- Water is routine; wine is exciting.
- Water is ordinary; wine is extraordinary.

Water represents the way that too many of us describe our relationship with God: *"Prayer is boring. Bible reading is*

---

[2] During the time of Jesus, drinking wine was not for the purpose of getting drunk. Drunkenness was actually seen as a great disgrace in Biblical times; it's too bad that had to change.

tedious. Church is lifeless. My spiritual life is dry. I'm just going through the motions, but not really experiencing anything special."

Wine, however, represents the way that *God* wants us to describe our relationship: *"Prayer is heartfelt. Bible reading is exciting. Church is life-changing. I am passionate about my spiritual life, and I feel like I have a deep connection with God. I'm living the joy-filled, abundant life Jesus promised."*

Too many of us have accepted subpar Christian lives; we are living like that felucca driver from earlier, and have become content with the way things are. Our spiritual lives are dry. Our marriages are stale. Our friendships are superficial. Going to church doesn't fire us up like it used to; sermons don't speak to us as powerfully as they do to everyone else. Everyone says we're supposed to be full of hope, full of joy, and full of peace, but the reality is we are living in confusion, in loneliness, and in despair.

Simply put, the wine has run out. We're running on water.

The question now becomes this: What are you going to do about it? Are you content with water? Or are you going to fight for wine?

THE SOLUTION: ASK & OBEY

At the wedding of Cana, Jesus wasn't content to just have water at the party; He wanted wine, and He also wanted the guests to have wine. Jesus is never content with ordinary, boring, dry, and lifeless water: HE WANTS WINE! And He was willing to do something about it.

Now it's your turn to do something about it, too. But what can *you* do? Isn't this something only Jesus can do?

Remember the math lesson from earlier? Some people will say: *"1 + 1 = 2. To go from water to wine, I need to pray more, read the Bible more, go to church more, give more, fast more, and stop throwing trash over the fence and into my neighbor's yard."*

Those are the "1 + 1" people.

Others will say: *"0 + infinity = infinity. There's nothing I can do; it's all in God's hands, and He'll make it wine when He wants to. Nothing for me to do other than wait patiently."*

Those are the "0 + infinity" people.

But we know that the formula for success is "5 + 2 = 5000." We offer our best and we trust God to do the rest.

Look back at John 2. What did the servants do? Which group did they fall into?

> Now there were set there six waterpots of stone, according to the manner of purification of the Jews, containing twenty or thirty gallons apiece. Jesus said to them, "Fill the waterpots with water." And they filled them up to the brim. And He said to them, "Draw some out now, and take it to the master of the feast." And they took it. (John 2:6-8)

If they were "1 + 1" people, they would have picked some grapes off the vine, tossed their shoes off, and started stomping the grapes to try to make their own wine. They wouldn't have gotten much, but a little is better than nothing, right?

If they were "0 + infinity" people, they would have responded to Jesus's request of *"fill the waterpots with water"* by saying, *"Why should we? If You're going to do a miracle anyway, then You might as well make wine out of nothing. Why do you need us to carry these heavy pitchers back and forth with water? Why don't You just make wine come from heaven and set it in front of the guests Yourself?"*

But thankfully they were "5 + 2" people. That's why the Bible says, *"They filled them up to the brim."* They did the best they could with what they had. They offered their best, and then humbly trusted God to do the rest.

And that's why they witnessed a miracle. That's why they saw water turn into wine.

The same formula applies to you as well. What do you do when the wine runs out in your marriage? What do you do when there's no joy in your heart? What do you do when serving God and worshiping God seem more like a chore than a blessing?

You do the two things those servants at the wedding did:

1. You ask for help.

The servants needed help. They had no hope of making wine on their own. It wouldn't matter if you gave them more time, or more waterpots, or more servants. It wasn't a matter of them needing *more* resources, it was a matter of them being physically unable to do it on their own.

They needed help, and they asked for it from Jesus.

The same holds true for us. We can't transform water into wine. No matter how hard we try or what we do, it's impossible. Those servants could have tried for 10 minutes or 10 years, and it wouldn't have made a difference. Only God can transform water into wine.

In what areas do you need God's help? Where is it that you've run up against a wall? What change have you been trying to make, but you just can't seem to do it?

Ask for help. Only God can turn water into wine.

2. Do whatever He tells you.

> His mother said to the servants, "Whatever He says
> to you, do it." (John 2:5)

Jesus told the servants to fill the waterpots, and they did it. Did this make sense to the servants?

> Jesus said to them, "Fill the waterpots with water."
> And they filled them up to the brim. (John 2:7)

Jesus told the servants to offer what was in the waterpots (which as far as they know is still water) to the master of the feast. Does that seem like a good idea?

> And He said to them, "Draw some out now, and
> take it to the master of the feast." And they took it.
> (John 2:8)

The bottom line is that this is not a "1 + 1 = 2" thing; it's a "5 + 2 = 5000" thing. That means that there will be some steps along the way that don't "add up" *(pun intended)*. Our job isn't to analyze what He says, or to understand what He says, or even to *agree* with what He says. Our job is to OBEY what He says.

In trying to find wine in your marriage, you might hear, *"Humble yourself."* In trying to find wine in your prayer life, you might hear, *"Get up early."* In trying to find wine in your career, you might hear, *"Stop stealing pencils and Post-its from the supply closet."*

Here's some great advice: *"Whatever He says to you, do it."*

OUR PRIVATE WINE MAKER

Two thousand years ago, there was a wedding in Cana and Jesus was there. And because He was there, a great miracle took place: Water turned into wine. Ordinary turned into extraordinary. Natural became supernatural.

And that was just the start. If you follow the rest of Jesus's ministry on earth, you'll see that transforming the ordinary into extraordinary was His specialty.

He took a woman who lived an adulterous life, and turned her into an evangelist. (See John 4.)

He took a tax collector and a traitor, and turned him into a devoted disciple. (See Luke 5.)

He took a murderer and a terrorist, and turned him into the author of half of the New Testament. (See Acts 9.)

That was His specialty: transforming old into new, ordinary into extraordinary, water into wine.

Today, we don't have Jesus with us like they did back at the wedding of Cana, but we have something better. (Go back three chapters if you've forgotten already.)

> Do you not know that you are the temple of
> God and that the Spirit of God dwells in you?
> (1 Corinthians 3:16)

The Spirit of God—aka, the Holy Spirit—lives within us. We are His temple and dwelling place. He is inside of us right now.

This means that we have access to a miracle every single day. Every day can be like the wedding of Cana because every day we have the full power of God within us. Every day we can a) ask for help, and b) do whatever He tells us.

Does that mean that we'll never see defeat again? We'll never be discouraged again? We'll never find ourselves struggling anymore?

No, but it means that we may start seeing some of that water turn into wine.

> But if the Spirit of Him who raised Jesus from the dead dwells in you, He who raised Christ from the dead will also give life to your mortal bodies through His Spirit who dwells in you. (Romans 8:11)

So, the next time you're feeling dry, or weighed down, or like you're just going through the motions, stop and ask for help. Ask the Holy Spirit—your personal Paraclete/Helper— to transform your time of prayer, from water into wine . . . or your Bible reading, from water into wine . . . or your workday, from water into wine.

Ask in full sincerity of heart, and then be prepared to do whatever He tells you to do—no matter what it is. Trust that God has done this before, and that He knows what He's doing.

And when we do that, eventually we'll find ourselves saying the same thing the wedding host said two thousand years ago:

> "You have kept the good wine until now!" (John 2:10)

God doesn't just give wine, He gives the best wine. And it's time for us to start tasting it.

197

PART FIVE

NOW IT'S YOUR TURN

I started this book by making a promise. I told you God has a special plan for your life—one that is exceedingly abundantly above all that you can ever imagine. And I promised you that saying *"whatever"* to God's plan would be the best decision you'd ever make.

It certainly was for me. Remember, I've lived on both sides of the fence: the *"don't-get-too-close-to-God-because-He-might-ruin-your-life"* side and the *"I-can't-get-enough-of-God-in-my-life"* side as well. I've tasted life with God, and life without God. I've been the guy sitting by the edge of the "God pool," just dipping my toes in, and I've been the guy doing cannonballs into the deep end as well.

I've been on both sides, and trust me, there's NO COMPARISON. It's not even close. Life *with* God beats life *without* God every single time. No contest.

But now it's time for you to go from reading about my experience to creating your own. It's time for all this information to be put to use, so you can take the next step in your relationship with God. You've hopefully gotten to know a lot *ABOUT* God through the course of this book, but now it's time to go from knowing about Him to actually *knowing* Him.

It's time to move from knowledge to experience. And the key to doing this is that tiny little word that I opened this book with . . . *"whatever."*

Saying *"whatever"* to God will open new doors of blessing, and unlock hidden treasures that God wants to pour into your life. That's what I wrote in the first section of this book:

"[God] had a plan for my life, but I just couldn't see it all those years. It wasn't until I accepted His plan—even though I didn't know what it would contain at the time—that He started to reveal it to me. And I'd be lying if I said I got it all figured out now. Not even close! God will continue to unveil more and more of His plan as long as I continue to say 'whatever' to it."

Now it's your turn. It's your turn to trust God and His plan for your life. It's your turn to take a step of faith and walk in obedience to God's commands. It's your turn to dive headfirst into the deep end of a relationship with God.

Now it's your turn to say, *"Whatever, God."*

CHAPTER 19

WHERE DO I START?

*I*f you've gotten this far, then I assume you're ready to jump in and start living a *"Whatever, God"* life for yourself. Good for you! I'm proud of you, and more importantly, I'm excited for you. I'm excited because I know that you're one giant step closer to experiencing a deep relationship with your Creator, the kind of relationship that can give long-lasting satisfaction and fulfillment to your life.

And if that's the case, then this final section may be the most important one yet. It's here that we'll discuss two essential principles of a life with God, and those principles will lead to what I call the two pillars of a *"Whatever, God"* life.

The pillars are like two legs when it comes to your relationship with God; the only way to move forward is to use them both. If you try to move one leg forward without the other, you'll only be able to get so far. You need both legs working together to keep making progress on your journey.

Enough with the introduction . . . GIVE US THE PRINCIPLES, ALREADY!

Principle #1: IF YOU WANT TO CARRY SOMETHING *BIG*, YOU MUST FIRST LET GO OF WHAT'S IN YOUR HAND.

I learned this principle several years ago at a weekend retreat for our church's high school girls. The topic of the retreat was the tabernacle of the Old Testament: the structure that God commanded the Israelites to build as His dwelling place. To set the mood for the retreat, we built a life-size model of one of the pieces of furniture in the tabernacle, the Ark of the Covenant. It was basically a big wooden box—4 feet long x 2 feet high x 2 feet deep—that looked very much like an old treasure chest.

As was my custom, I arrived at the retreat center early. I unpacked my bags, set up the lecture hall, and began waiting patiently for the girls to arrive. As soon as they arrived, I began unloading their luggage from the bus.

I was in a hurry to finish because a) it was late, b) it was dark, and c) I was hungry! So I got into "maximum efficiency mode" and tried to carry as much as I could, in as few trips as possible. I was putting multiple backpacks on each shoulder, sleeping bags under my arms, pillows on top of my head . . . whatever I could do to finish quicker. I wasn't going for style points here; I just wanted to finish.

And that meant trying to carry as many items as I possibly could at the same time. *(Remember this point; lesson coming soon.)*

Then it came time to carry the Ark of the Covenant, that big, bulky wooden box. I figured I could put some backpacks around my shoulders, put a couple of sleeping bags on top of the Ark, and then carry it all into the cabin at the same time.

Just call me Mr. Efficiency!

But there was a problem. When I bent down to pick up the Ark, the backpacks all slid off. So, I tried again—this time leaning a bit to one side so they wouldn't fall off. I got a little bit closer, but again it didn't work. The third time I tried to pick up the Ark with just one hand, and press it against my body, but again, I failed.

Picture the scene: Here I was trying to carry this big wooden box, while at the same time, trying to balance two backpacks on one shoulder. Every time I bent down to pick up the box, the bags fell. I repositioned the bags a different way and tried again, and failed again. And then I tried using one hand, and that didn't work either. I tried everything I could think of, and nothing worked.

Then one young lady came to me—a sophomore in high school, sent by God to teach me a lesson—and said, *"Fr. Anthony, if you want to carry that box, I think you need to put down the other bags first."*

BRILLIANT! Absolutely brilliant!

That was the origin of principle #1: *If you want to carry something BIG, you must first let go of what's in your hand.*

I started off carrying one thing (backpacks), and then I decided I wanted to carry something else (a big wooden box). But I didn't want to carry that new thing *INSTEAD* of the old thing; I wanted to carry the new thing *IN ADDITION* to the old thing.

But that didn't work. It was too much. I needed both hands and both shoulders free in order to carry something as big as that wooden box. I didn't have the capacity to carry the box while still holding on to the other things. It was too big to just fit in my pocket or carry with one hand. If I was going to carry this box, I needed to start letting go of some of the other things I was holding on to.

And the most ironic part of this story is what the box symbolized. It was a symbol of God's Presence! The box represented God Himself!

The lesson is crystal clear: If you want to live a new life with God, you must let go of your old life first. You can't carry both. Life with God isn't something small; you can't hold on to it and hold on to your old life at the same time. Some things are going to have to go.

It's like getting married. When you decide to get married, you know that you have to let go of some things first—like dating other girls, and living in your parents' house, and burping any time you want. If you want to start a new life in marriage, you need to let go of your old life as a single person.

Why? *Because if you want to carry something BIG, you must first let go of what's in your hand.*

The same applies to a relationship with God. If you want a new life *with* God, you must first let go of your old life *without* God. You can't just *squeeze* God in and make Him fit into the spare parts of your life. Some things are going to have to change; some parts are going to need to go.

And that leads us to the first pillar in the *"Whatever, God"* life:

PILLAR #1: REPENTANCE

"Repentance is not a confession of sins but a change of mind." —Tertullian

The word *"repent"* may be the single most important word in the entire New Testament. It conveys the essential requirement upon which a relationship with God must be built.

> John [the Baptist] came baptizing in the wilderness and preaching a baptism of REPENTANCE for the remission of sins. (Mark 1:4)

> From that time Jesus began to preach and to say, "REPENT, for the kingdom of heaven is at hand." (Matthew 4:17)

> So they went out and preached that people should REPENT. (Mark 6:12)

> Truly, these times of ignorance God overlooked, but now commands all men everywhere to REPENT. (Acts 17:30)

The word *"repent"* comes from the Greek word *"metanoia,"* which means *"a change of mind"* or *"a change of heart."* To repent means to make a fundamental conversion in the way one thinks and lives.

We often confuse repentance with a feeling of sorrow or grief or regret; we think *"to repent"* means *"to feel bad about my sins."* But that isn't it at all. It's much more than a feeling; repentance is an action . . . it's a change. Feelings may be part of the repentance process, but there's certainly much more to it than that.

When Jesus called us to repent (see earlier verses), was He calling us just to feel sorry for our mistakes? Was John the Baptist preaching a "baptism of *regret* for the remission of sins"? In Acts 17, was the Apostle Paul commanding *all men everywhere to FEEL BAD about their sins?*

Of course not! They weren't calling us to feel bad about our sinful ways, they were calling us to CHANGE our sinful ways. They were directing us to change our fundamental view of sin and its consequences. They were inviting us to *let go* of something old, in order to *lay hold* of something new.

> "Repent, and turn from all your transgressions, so that iniquity will not be your ruin. Cast away from you all the transgressions which you have committed, and get yourselves a new heart and a new spirit." (Ezekiel 18:30-31)

Repentance means to give up our old ways—our old thought patterns, our old sinful habits, our old unforgiving attitudes. We are called to let go of those old ways and to leave them behind. That's the only way for God to bless us and give us new ways.

He can't give us new thought patterns if we're still holding on to our old thought patterns. He can't help us establish new habits if we're still holding on to our old habits. He can't give us new hearts and new attitudes if we refuse to let go of our old ones.

That doesn't mean that we become perfect and don't make mistakes anymore. Not at all! Repentance doesn't mean that we sin no more, it means we *strive* to sin no more. It means that we've realized the error of our ways, and we've made a true *"change of mind."* We no longer see our sin as harmless and insignificant; instead we see it for what it is—a deadly disease that threatens our relationship with God.

That's why repentance isn't just a one-time thing. You don't just repent today, and then you're done. Repentance is like brushing your teeth; no matter how well you cleaned them yesterday, you still need to brush today as well.

Repentance is a daily decision to let go of the things that are hindering you from growing closer to God. It's letting go of what's in my hand, so I can hold on to something much bigger and much greater.

So what are you holding on to? What are you carrying today that's stopping you from being able to fully grab hold of God and a deep relationship with Him? A bitter heart? An unforgiving attitude? A selfish habit? A destructive addiction? A sinful relationship?

Think back to that picture of me at the high school girls' retreat. What's stopping you from holding on to God with both hands?

Whatever it is, it's time to REPENT.

Principle #2: "GOD-THINGS" CAN'T BE DONE WITH "MAN-POWER."

Some things aren't a matter of effort. Some things just can't be done. Fish can't fly. Birds can't swim. Ducks can't hop. No matter how hard they try, none of them will ever be able to accomplish those feats. They just can't do them.

Or can they?

I can put a fish on a plane, and it'll fly across the sky. I can put a bird in a cage, and put the cage on a boat, and the bird will think it's swimming across the ocean. I can put that duck in my backpack, and jump on a trampoline for an hour, and that duck will feel like a kangaroo.

So maybe I need to revise my earlier statement. Instead of saying they *can't* do it, let me instead say they can't do it *on their own.* They need help; they need someone bigger than themselves.

In the same way, as human beings, we aren't able to do God-things. We can't turn water into wine *(both literally and figuratively)*. We can't calm our fears. We can't remove the temptations around us. We can't inject ourselves with a dose of discipline and self-control.

Those are what I call God-things, and we simply aren't able to do them . . .

. . . or rather, we aren't able to do them *on our own.*

Like the animal examples, we just need a little help from someone bigger than ourselves.

Living the abundant life is a God-thing. Having God work all things together for good is a God-thing too. Receiving guidance and correction and help from the Holy Spirit . . . those are all God-things as well. Only God can do them, and if He chooses not to, they simply aren't going to get done.

> Did you receive the Spirit by the works of the law, or by the hearing of faith? Are you so foolish? Having begun in the Spirit, are you now being made perfect by the flesh? (Galatians 3:2-3)

Here, the Apostle Paul is being a bit sarcastic with the Galatians. He's saying, *"What's going on here, guys? What happened to you? Do you think that God gave you His Spirit because you earned it? Are you that foolish? You used to know that it was only by His goodness and graciousness that you received His Spirit, but are you now going around telling people that it's because of your efforts?"*

You see, at first the devil tries to get us to live in sin. He tries to make us love sin and remain in sin forever. But once we've addressed that issue with the pillar of repentance, he doesn't leave us alone; he simply moves to plan B. When he sees that we're striving to live a godly life and pursuing a deeper relationship with God, he'll simply switch over to the deception of *SELF-EFFORT*.

The deception of self-effort is when we start attributing God-things to our own efforts. We're like the fish in the airplane, who is flying over the mountains and thinking that it's all because he was kind to his fish neighbor—and because he let his neighbor eat that last fish flake at feeding time this morning.

That's the deception of self-effort.

As much as the devil would love to get you to live in sin, he'd be just as happy to have you attribute the God-things in your life to your own efforts. It's like driving down a road with a ditch on both sides. If he can't push you in on one side, he'll be happy to push you in on the other. It doesn't really matter to him; all that matters is that you're in a ditch.

So what do we do? We move to the second pillar of a *"Whatever, God"* life.

PILLAR #2: FAITH

The perfect example of this pillar comes in the famous story of the Samaritan woman, also known as the Woman at the Well, which appears in John 4.

Jesus meets a woman who knows a little bit about God, but clearly yearns for more. She meets Jesus, and despite not knowing too much about God, she realizes that she's being offered something big—a God-thing—and she wants to figure out how to get it.

> Jesus answered and said to her "If you knew the gift of God, and who it is who says to you, 'Give Me a drink,' you would have asked Him, and He would have given you living water." (John 4:10)

211

Jesus offers her *"living water."* That's the God-thing in this story. Something divine, something from heaven, something that she can't produce on her own. And how does she respond?

> The woman said to Him, "Sir, You have nothing to draw with, and the well is deep. Where then do You get that living water?" (John 4:11)

He's talking about the gift of God, and she's talking about buckets! He's saying, *"I have something amazing to give you, something you could never get on your own."* She responds, *"Great, but I think we're going to need a bigger bucket."*

Bucket?! What bucket?! We're not talking about water that goes in a bucket! We're talking about a God-thing, something that's bigger than buckets . . . something that you can't get on your own.

That's where the second pillar comes in.

Like repentance, faith is another one of those misunderstood words. We often think of faith as "blind belief" or some type of "godly optimism." We think people who have faith are people who always see the glass half full.

But faith isn't so much about *WHAT* we believe, but rather *IN WHOM* we believe. The question isn't whether or not you have faith; the question is who or what is your faith in? Is it in yourself and your own efforts? Or is your faith in God and His grace?

At the start of the story, the Samaritan woman had faith, but it wasn't in Jesus—it was in herself and in her efforts. She believed that she needed to work harder and do more to get this *"living water"* that Jesus told her about. That's why she responded how she did at the beginning.

But by the end of the story, things changed significantly. Jesus has a lengthy dialogue with her and walks her through the first pillar of repentance. He then tells her that He is the Messiah, and challenges her to put her faith in Him.

Then we read this:

> The woman then left her waterpot, went her way into the city, and said to the men, "Come, see a Man who told me all things that I ever did. Could this be the Christ?" Then they went out of the city and came to Him. (John 4:28-30)

Notice what she did: She left her waterpot. Why? She stopped believing the lie of self-effort. She realized that she did not have the ability to get this water on her own, no matter how many buckets she had or what size they were. She needed someone bigger than herself. She needed God.

So she left her waterpot and put her faith in Jesus.

How about you? Be honest. Where are you putting your trust? In yourself and in your bucket? Or in someone bigger? Are you the fish sitting in first class, thinking that it's all because of your efforts? Or are you the woman at the well, leaving aside her means of sustenance (the waterpot), and placing all her faith in the Lord Jesus?

We all have faith in something. We all trust in something to get results. The question isn't whether you have faith; the real question is whom or what are you placing your faith in?

YOUR STARTING LINE: REPENTANCE & FAITH

The starting point of a new life with God is repentance and faith. Those are the two pillars that you need to build your relationship with God upon. Every day should have repentance: metanoia or change, and every day should have faith: placing your trust in someone bigger than yourself.

> Therefore, leaving the discussion of the elementary principles of Christ, let us go on to perfection, not laying again the foundation of repentance from dead works and of faith toward God. (Hebrews 6:1)

It's time to start your journey to that new life today. Here's how you do it:

1) Set aside a chunk of time—as much time as you can, at least 10-15 minutes. Get a Bible, a notepad, and a pen.
2) Examine your life. Where are you falling short? Where are you holding on to something that's keeping you from God? Is it a relationship? A habit? An attitude? Ask yourself what's holding you back. Write it down.
3) Strengthen your faith in God. Humble yourself and remember that He's God and you're not. Remind yourself that you can't do this alone. You need God, and if He's not a part of the solution, then you're going to be in trouble.
4) Read Psalm 25. It's one of the prayers that King David said as he practiced these two pillars as well.
5) Tell someone else about your experience. You don't need to share all the details, but make sure to tell at least one person that you're serious about your relationship with God and that you want to make a change.

Now is your chance. Don't wait for tomorrow. God is inviting you to come deeper and know Him more intimately, and the starting point is repentance and faith.

And if you're still not convinced, I have one more story that might change your mind . . .

CHAPTER **20**

AN OFFER YOU CAN'T REFUSE

*T*here's a famous story that's been used in Sunday school classrooms for generations that illustrates perfectly what a *"Whatever, God"* life is all about. It's the tale of a five-year-old girl named Jenny and her beautiful pearl necklace.

The story begins with Jenny and her mother going to the mall and seeing a toy pearl necklace on sale for $4.99. Jenny falls in love with the necklace and begs her mother to buy it for her. But Jenny's mother tells her if she wants to buy it, she has to earn the money and buy it herself. Jenny loves the necklace so much, and she is determined to find a way.

So, she starts doing extra chores around the house. She collects loose change from underneath the couch cushions. She even opens a lemonade stand right outside her grandma's house, knowing that she'll have at least one faithful customer there.

She works and works and works—and eventually she does it! She earns enough money for the necklace. Jenny and her mother go back to the mall, and Jenny buys the toy necklace. She did it! She now has the very thing that she's wanted for so long! YES!

Jenny loves her new pearl necklace and she doesn't hide it. She wears it everywhere she goes. You can seldom find a moment where she isn't either wearing or playing with her necklace. She absolutely loves it!

And then one night, her father comes into her room before bedtime and asks her, *"Jenny, do you trust me?"*

Jenny replies, *"Of course I do, Daddy. I trust you sooooooo much!"*

"Then I'd like you to give me your pearl necklace, Jenny," replies the father.

"Oh no, Daddy! No, no, no! Anything but the pearl necklace. Here, you can take my stuffed animals or my roller skates . . . you can have anything you want, but please don't ask for my pearl necklace," cries Jenny.

The father accepts her answer, gives her a kiss on the fore-head, and says, *"You know I love you, Jenny. Good night."*

One week later, he comes into her room again and asks the same thing, *"Jenny, do you trust me?"*

"Of course I do, Daddy," answers Jenny.

"Then I want you to give me your pearl necklace," says the father.

"No, Daddy, no! Please, please, please don't take my neck-lace from me. You can have anything else, but please don't make me give up my pearl necklace," cries Jenny.

Once again, he accepts her answer, gives her another kiss on the forehead, and says, *"You know I love you, Jenny. Good night."*

A few days later, he comes into her room again, but this time he finds Jenny crying as he enters.

"What's wrong, Jenny? Why are you crying?" he asks.

"Here, Daddy. Take it," says Jenny as she unclenches her fist and releases her beloved pearl necklace into her father's hand. *"I know you want me to give you my pearl necklace. I don't know why you'd ask me to do this because you know that it's my favorite thing ever . . . but, I trust you. Here . . . you can have it."*

The father, now with tears in his eyes as well, takes Jenny's fake pearl necklace and puts it in his left pocket. He then reaches into his right pocket with his other hand, pulls out a small velvet box, and gives it to Jenny. He tells her that this is her gift for trusting him.

Jenny opens the box and discovers that inside is a REAL PEARL NECKLACE!

He'd had it in his pocket the whole time and had been trying to give it to her since the day he saw her with the fake pearls. He knew that the fake pearls wouldn't really satisfy her; he knew that they would provide short-term satisfaction at best. He wanted her to have the real pearls that would satisfy her for life.

And every night, when he'd enter her room, he intended to give her the real pearls; he was just waiting for her to let go of the fake ones and to trust him.

AN OFFER YOU CAN'T REFUSE

Like Jenny, I believe your Father is ready to give you something great as well. He's ready to give you something that will satisfy you and fulfill you in a way that you have never even imagined. He's ready to give you a new life . . . an abundant life . . . an exceedingly abundantly, above all that we can imagine life . . . a life where all things work together for good, and a life where every day is wine, not water.

As a Father, that is God's greatest desire. He wants to give you that life, even more than you want to receive it.

"Do not fear, little flock, for it is your Father's **good pleasure** to give you the kingdom." (Luke 12:32)

But He can't give it to you if you don't trust Him. He can't give it to you if you aren't willing to let go of what's in your hand and have faith that He has something better.

That's the basis of a *"Whatever, God"* life. It's knowing the character of God *(God is real, God is relevant, and God is rewarding)* and trusting that what God gives will always be better than what you have. It's trusting that a life with God beats a life without God every single time.

It's looking to God, with a heart full of trust, and saying *"WHATEVER, GOD."*

Conclusion

FINAL THOUGHTS

I said at the start of this book that my goal is to help you see where God wants you to be . . . how He wants you to live . . . and what your life should look like and could look like if you allowed Him to lead it for you.

My hope is that this book is to you what *"the star in the East"* was to a group of wise men two thousand years ago *(see Matthew 2:1-12)*. The star appeared out of nowhere, and disappeared almost as quickly, but in the meantime, it did its job. It led people to Jesus. It helped them find God.

We often commend those wise men for seeking God and being willing to travel so far to find Him. But I see it a little differently. I don't see that they were seeking God as much as God was seeking them. That's why He sent them the star— because He wanted to be found, even more than they wanted to find Him.

I trust that if you're seeking God today, then He'll use this book as a star in your life. And I also trust that there will be many more stars to come into your life, each one drawing you a little closer to your Father in heaven.

"And you will seek Me and find Me, when you search for Me with all your heart." (Jeremiah 29:13)

www.ingramcontent.com/pod-product-compliance
Lightning Source LLC
Chambersburg PA
CBHW020926090426
42736CB00010B/1051

* 9 7 8 0 6 4 8 5 7 5 4 9 8 *